Crossway

Series editors: Ian Coffey (NT), Stephen Gaukroger (OT)
New Testament editor: Stephen Motyer

Also in this series

Dedication

For all the women in my life:
Hazel, Ruth, Helen, Elspeth,
Lydia, Eleanor and Anna

John's gospel: Crossway Bible Guide

Ian Barclay

Crossway Books Leicester

CROSSWAY BOOKS
38 De Montfort Street, Leicester LE1 7GP, England

First published 1997

The author thanks David Stone for his preparation of the discussion
questions in this Bible Guide.

British Library Cataloguing in Publication Data

A catalogue record for this book is available from
the British Library

ISBN 1–85684–165–0

Set in Palatino

Typeset in Great Britain by Parker Typesetting Service, Leicester
Printed in Great Britain by The Guernsey Press Co. Ltd, Guernsey,
Channel Islands

CONTENTS

These days, meeting together to study the Bible appears to be a booming leisure-time activity in many parts of the world. In the United Kingdom alone, it is estimated that over one million people each week meet in home Bible-study groups.

This series has been designed to help such groups and, in particular, those who lead them, but it is are also eminently suitable for individual study. We are also aware of the needs of those who preach and teach to larger groups as well as the hard-pressed student, all of whom often look for a commentary that gives a concise summary and lively application of a particular passage.

We have therefore enlisted authors who are in the business of teaching the Bible to others and are doing it well. They have kept in their sights two clear aims:

1. To explain and apply the message of the Bible in non-technical language.
2. To encourage discussion, prayer and action on what the Bible teaches.

All of us engaged in the project believe that the Bible is the Word of God – given to us in order that people might discover him and his purposes for our lives. We believe that the sixty-six books which go to make up the Bible, although written by different people, in different places, at different times, through different circumstances, have a single unifying theme: that theme is Salvation. This means free forgiveness and the removal of all our guilt, it means the gift of eternal life, and it means the wholeness of purpose and joy which God has designed us to experience here and now, all of this being made possible through the Lord Jesus Christ.

How to use this Bible Guide

These guides have been prepared both for personal study and for the leaders and members of small groups. More information about group study follows on the next few pages.

You can use this book very profitably as a personal study guide. The short studies are ideal for daily reading: the first of the questions is usually aimed to help you with personal reflection (see *How to tackle personal Bible study*). If you prefer to settle down to a longer period of study you can use groups of three to five studies, and thus get a better overview of a longer Bible passage. In either case using the Bible Guide will help you to be disciplined about regular study, a habit that countless Christians have found greatly beneficial. (See also *How to tackle John's gospel* for methods of selecting studies if you do not intend to use them all.)

Yet a third use for these Bible Guides is as a quarry for ideas for the busy Bible teacher, providing outlines and application for those giving talks or sermons or teaching children. You will need more than this book can offer of course, but the way the Bible text is broken down, comments offered and questions raised may well suggest directions to follow.

How to tackle personal Bible study

We have already suggested that you might use this book as a personal study guide. Now for some more detail.

One of the best methods of Bible study is to read the text through carefully several times, possibly using different versions or translations. Having reflected on the material it is a good discipline to write down your own thoughts before doing anything else. At this stage the introduction of other books can be useful. If you are using this book as your main study resource, then read through the relevant sections carefully, turning up the Bible references that are mentioned. The questions at the end of each chapter are specifically designed to help you to apply the passage to your own situation. You may find it helpful to write your answers to the questions in your notes.

It is a good habit to conclude with prayer, bringing before God the things you have learned.

If this kind of in-depth study is too demanding for you and you have only a short time at your disposal, read the Bible passage, read the comments in the Bible Guide, think round one of the questions and commit what you have learned to God in a brief prayer. This would take about fifteen minutes without rushing it.

How to tackle your group Bible study

1. Getting help

If you are new to leading groups you will obviously want to get all the help you can from ministers and experienced friends. Books are also extremely helpful and we strongly recommend a book prepared by the editors of this series of Bible Guides: *Housegroups: the leaders' survival guide*, edited by Ian Coffey and Stephen Gaukroger (Crossway Books, 1996). This book looks at the whole range of different types of group, asking what is the point of it all, what makes a good leader, how to tackle your meeting, how to help the members, how to study, pray, share, worship and plenty of other pointers, tips and guidelines.

This book is a 'must' for all leaders of small groups. It is written by a team of people widely experienced in this area. It is available at your local Christian bookshop. If you have difficulty in obtaining a copy write to Crossway Books, Norton Street, Nottingham, NG7 3HR, UK.

2. Planning a programme with your Bible Guide

This guide is a commentary on God's Word, written to help a group to get the most out of their studies. Although it is never ideal to chop up Scripture into small pieces, which the authors never intended, huge chunks are indigestible and we have tried to provide a diet of bite-sized mouthfuls.

The book is divided into major parts, each with a title indicated by a part-title page with a large number. If you want to get an overview of the Bible book in a series of meetings you will need to select appropriate studies for each meeting. Read them yourself first and prepare a short summary of the studies you are tackling for your group. Ideally you could write it on a sheet of A5 paper and hand a copy to each member.

Then choose one study from the part you are dealing with as a basis for your meeting. Do not attempt to pack more than one study into one meeting but choose the crucial one, the study which best crystallizes the message. There are examples in *How to tackle John's gospel* below.

If you do not intend to cover the whole Bible book, choose a series of studies to suit the number of meetings you have available. Each part of the commentary is divided into a few (usually 3–5) studies. If you have an eight-week programme with weekly meetings you could aim to cover two parts of the book. It is a good idea to use consecutive studies, not to dodge about. You will then build up a detailed picture of one section of Scripture. Alternative examples of programmes of study for this book are given in *How to tackle John's gospel*.

3. Resources

You will find any or all of these books of great value in providing background to your Bible knowledge. Put some of them on your Christmas list and build up your library.

New Bible Dictionary or *New Concise Bible Dictionary* (IVP)
New Bible Atlas (IVP)

New Bible Commentary (21st Century edition) (IVP)
Handbook of Life in Bible Times: John Thompson (IVP)
The Bible User's Manual (IVP)
The Lion Handbook to the Bible (Lion Publishing)
The Message of the Bible (Lion Publishing)
NIV Study Bible (Hodder & Stoughton)
The Bible with Pleasure: Stephen Motyer (Crossway Books)

The relevant volume in the IVP Tyndale Commentary series will give you reliable and detailed help with any knotty points you may encounter.

4. Preparing to lead

Reading, discussing with friends, studying, praying, reflecting on life . . . preparation can be endless. But do not be daunted by that. If you wait to become the perfect leader you will never start at all. The really vital elements in preparation are:

▶ prayer (not only in words but an attitude of dependence on God, 'Lord, I can't manage this on my own')

▶ familiarity with the study passage (careful reading of the text, the Bible Guide study and any other resource books that throw light on it) and

▶ a clear idea of where you hope to get in the meeting (notes on your introduction, perhaps, recap what was covered at the last meeting, and what direction you hope the questions will take you in – don't force the group to give your answers).

Here is a short checklist for the busy group leader:

Have I prayed about the meeting?
Have I decided exactly what I want to achieve through the meeting?
Have I prepared the material?
Am I clear about the questions that will encourage positive group discussion?

Am I gently encouraging silent members?

Am I, again gently, quietening the chatterers?

Am I willing to admit ignorance?

Am I willing to listen to what the group says and to value their contributions?

Am I ready not to be dogmatic, not imposing my ideas on the group?

Have I planned how to involve the group in discovering for themselves?

Have I developed several 'prayer points' that will help focus the group?

Are we applying Scripture to our experience of real life or only using it as a peg to hang our opinions on?

Are we finding resources for action and change or just having a nice talk?

Are we all enjoying the experience together?

How to tackle *John's gospel*

Now let's assume you are planning an eight-week course of studies (you will have to make the adjustments if you have more or fewer meetings). Where do you begin? This is entirely up to you and your group of course but, to get you started, here are a few possible routes you might take in a brief survey of the whole book.

There is so much in the book of *John* that no short series of eight studies could properly represent its message. However, eight sessions are better than none at all. You may wish to make your own selection (being careful to avoid bias in your choice). Do not select all the readings on the Holy Spirit nor concentrate exclusively on evangelism nor the battle between backward-looking Jews and the new faith, unless of course one of these is a specific focus for your study. But beware of pretending that any one narrow theme represents the book as a whole. Here are several possible selections.

1. Miracles of Jesus

Water becomes wine   2:1–11
Harvest and healing   4:31–54
The healing at the pool   5:1–15
The loaves and the fish   6:1–15
Jesus walks on water   6:16–28
Light for a blind man   9:1–23
The disciples meet the risen Lord   20:19–31

2. Celebrated extracts from the gospel

Jesus enters his own creation   1:6–18
Nicodemus   3:1–15
The woman at the well   4:1–15
The adulterous woman   8:1–11
Light for a blind man   9:1-23
The entry into Jerusalem   12:12–19
The servant Jesus   13:1–17
Focus on the Holy Spirit   16:5–15

3. The 'I AM' sayings

Introduction: Jesus as God   1:1–15
The bread of life   6:29–71
The light of the world   8:12 (see also chapter 9)
The gate for the sheep   10:1–10
The good shepherd   10:11–18 (i.e. one study in two halves)
The resurrection and the life   11:17–57
The way, the truth and the life   14:1–14
The true vine   15:1–8

4. The Passion

Section 5, seven studies in John 18:1 – 20:31, would be suitable for
Lent and Easter.

These outlines are meant to be springboards for your own ideas,
so please do not follow them slavishly. Adapt them for your own

use, merge them or ignore them.

In any case much of John will go unread if you concentrate only on these short snippets. You as leader will need to read carefully the whole book so that you can refer your group to sections they have not read. It would be wise to read a whole chapter when studying a part of it – the context often throws light on the verses you are looking at.

What can we expect to learn from *John's gospel*?

▶ It helps us *find the way* to Christ.

▶ It gives us a clear picture of Jesus, as Son of God.

▶ It shows us what it means to be 'born again'.

▶ There is in-depth teaching on the Holy Spirit.

▶ We see what is expected of disciples today.

▶ We meet Jesus the creator and the reason for the existence of everything.

Finding your way round this book

In our Bible Guides we have developed special symbols to
make things easier to follow. Every study therefore has
an opening section which is the passage in a nutshell.

The main section is the one that *makes sense of
the passage*.

Questions

Every passage also has special questions for personal and group
study after the main section. Some questions are addressed to us
as individuals, some speak to us as members of our church or
home group, while others concern us as members of God's
people world-wide. The questions are deliberately designed:

▶ to get people thinking about the passage

▶ to apply the text to 'real life' situations

▶ to encourage reflection, discussion and action!

As a group leader you may well discover additional questions
that will have special relevance to your group, so look out for
these and note them in your preparation time.

Digging deeper

Some passages, however, require an extra amount of explanation, and we have put these sections into two categories. The first kind gives additional background material that helps us to understand something factual. For example, if we dig deeper into the gospels, it helps us to know who the Pharisees were, so that we can see more easily why they related to Jesus in the way they did. These technical sections are marked with a spade.

Important doctrines

The second kind of explanatory section appears with passages which have important doctrines contained in them and which we need to study in more depth if we are to grow as Christians. Special sections that explain them to us in greater detail are marked with a face as above.

Introducing *John's gospel*

The gospels are a unique literary form; there is nothing else like them. At first glance you might say, 'Oh this is a biography of Jesus Christ', but this is not so in our modern sense. They contain biographical material certainly. Early writer Justin Martyr (second century AD) described them as 'memoirs of the apostles'. To this has been added the teaching of Jesus. We know virtually nothing about him apart from what we are told in the gospels. Jesus himself didn't leave a written record. If he had done, it would probably have been much more like the writing of an Old Testament prophet and would be a mixture of personal detail intermingled with very direct sermon material (cf. Amos 7:10–17).

Each gospel writer records a personal account of the life of Jesus for the particular part of the early church that he is serving and to this he adds the teaching of Jesus. Jesus spoke in Aramaic (the local Hebrew dialect in Palestine) and the gospels were written in Greek (the official language of the eastern part of the Roman Empire).

John's gospel is different from the first three, which are often referred to as the 'common-view gospels' (synoptics); this could be because he is writing later. John leaves out important parts of the story (such as the account of Jesus' birth). This may be because he assumed his readers had read them already in one of the other three gospels. He is writing as a pastor, and his deep desire is that his readers should *find the way* to Christ (John 20:30).

JESUS ALWAYS WAS AND ALWAYS WILL BE

John 1:1–18

John 1:1-5

Jesus has always been God

John begins at the very root of all reality by showing us that God's spoken Word set the universe in motion.

Jesus was before everything (verses 1–2)

The first thing that John wants to do is to show us what Jesus was like before the world began. In two crisp sentences he declares that Jesus is God and that he was here before anything else was created. Behind these two sentences, John almost seems to be playing two signature tunes that would grab the attention of the people of his day and link Jesus with the two main cultural groups of the ancient world.

If John were alive today, you could imagine him playing the signature tunes of the 'soap operas' *Neighbours* and *EastEnders* to link Jesus with Australia and London. The two biblical tunes that he plays are:

1. 'In the beginning', which would immediately be recognized by Jewish people because they named the books of the Bible by their opening words. So 'In the beginning' would remind them of *Genesis* where God spoke and everything came into

existence. John is saying to those with a Jewish background that Jesus was God's spoken word who brought everything into being.

2. 'The Word', which would be recognized by all with a Greek background and would imply that he was the divine 'reason' behind everything.

So by saying, 'In the beginning was the Word' (verse 1), John cements these two cultural groups together and tells them both that Jesus is the divine reason behind everything and the one by whom everything was made.

Jesus is the creator of everything (verse 3)

'Through him all things were made' (verse 3). I saw a TV programme recently which spoke of our universe consisting of 100 million galaxies, with each one containing 100 billion stars. In the words of Graham Kendrick, it was the hands of Jesus who flung each one of them 'into space'.

Everything in the world was created by Jesus, whether we are looking at the vastness of the universe or the minuteness of the different parts of an atom. While we must be careful not to fall into the trap of elevating creation to an object of worship, as some modern movements do, we need to notice that these opening words of John are a 'green' statement. No part of creation should be wasted, or used and abused simply to satisfy our desires and greed.

Jesus is the life force behind everything (verses 4–5)

'In him was life, and that life was the light of men' (verse 4). 'Light' and 'life' are words that are universally used as religious symbols. Again John is taking us back to Genesis and implying that Jesus is the life-force behind everything. John develops this by pointing out that Jesus is always shining in the darkness and that darkness will never overcome him.

Sin and evil can't restrict or defeat Jesus in any way. The 'darkness' can never overcome Jesus; 'overcome' is probably a better word than 'understood' (verse 5).

Some time ago I took a party of teenagers on a midnight walk across the Isle of Wight. It was a beautifully clear summer night and we could see a good number of the 10 octillion stars in the sky. As we approached a hill it appeared that one of them had fallen out of the sky on to the path just ahead of us. I hurried forward and discovered a glow-worm. I scooped it up on to my pocket Bible and found I could actually read by the light that the little creature provided. All the deep darkness of space couldn't extinguish the light of one small glow-worm.

John is saying that all the hostile darkness in the fallen part of the universe will never be able to extinguish the incomparably greater 'light' and 'life' of Jesus Christ.

Questions

1. In what way are these verses a 'green' statement? How much effort should we put into looking after the physical world?
2. What does John mean by 'darkness' in these verses?
3. How does the light of Jesus overcome the darkness?

Great truth hidden in the grammar

In the first three verses of John's gospel there are two different verbs *to be*; this isn't immediately obvious in our translations. The word 'was' in verse 1 means *'always existing'*; while the same English word in verse 3 actually means *'came into created being'*. You could translate the first three verses of John's gospel:

In the beginning *always existing* was the Word, and the Word was *always existing* with God, and the Word was *always existing*

God. He was *always existing* with God in the beginning. Through him all created things came into *created being*, with him nothing came in *created being* that has *created being*.

John 1:6–18

Jesus enters his own creation

Jesus comes to reveal to us what God is like, what his plans are, and how we can be transformed into members of God's family.

We will deal with John the Baptizer (verses 6–9) later when we look at him in the next chapter.

'Jesus in our neighbourhood'

'He was in the world . . .' (verse 10). If you had managed to catch one of the disciples in the Jerusalem of Christ's day, and then asked him if there was any evidence that the God of the Jews had ever visited this planet, he would have said, 'Oh yes! When God led us out of Egypt to this promised land he was with us in the tent (tabernacle), his presence was demonstrated by a pillar of fire at night and a pillar of cloud by day' (Exodus 13:21).

Then the disciple's eyes might have lit up as he added, 'Try and catch sight of Jesus of Nazareth, because some of us think that God is again "tenting" (tabernacling) with us in Jesus Christ.' That is what John is saying. 'The Word became flesh and made his dwelling (tabernacle) among us' (verse 14). It was obviously a powerful picture for the early Jewish Christians; but how would you express it in English today? 'The Word became flesh ... and *bungalowed-with-us*'; or *'apartmented-with-us'*; or even *'semi-detached-with-us'*? One contemporary translation has it, 'The Word became flesh ... and moved into the neighbourhood'. It doesn't really matter how we say it, as long as we see the reality of the visit Jesus made to this planet.

To make us appreciate this, there is something almost crude in the way John expresses it. He doesn't say, 'Jesus became a human being' or even that he 'took a body'. But 'The Word became flesh'. John is saying that Jesus entered right into the heart of our bodily experience and therefore has an intimate knowledge of all the problems we face.

Jesus is able to transform us

'Yet to all who received him (Jesus), to all who believed in his name (who understand all that he is), he gave the right to become children of God' (verse 12). Notice three words: *gave*, *right* and *children*.

▶ *Gave*: John is writing about God's gift of salvation to mankind. As God offers this 'indescribable gift' in Christ (2 Corinthians 9:15), we can choose the tragedy of rejecting or the blessing of receiving. If we receive his gift, God welcomes us into his family.

▶ *Right*: Many translations say 'power' but perhaps 'authority' would be an even better word. Our Queen has the right, the power and authority to bestow honours. But John isn't talking about a monarch who rules a country, he is speaking of the King of Kings and Lord of Lords, the one who rules the universe and who obviously has authority to make us part of his family, should he choose to do so. In the old translation of the Bible there are long lists of 'begats'. When we receive Christ we are 'born of (begotten by) God' (verse 13).

▶ *Children*: To be made part of God's family is to be made a very special person. The corollary of this is that everybody else who has received Christ is also special. There are, therefore, no ordinary people in God's family. This means we must start to treat other Christians in the right way; not only those in our own fellowship but also all truly converted believers, whatever their tradition.

The enormous resources of Jesus to bless

'From the fulness of his grace we have all received one blessing after another' (verse 16). The sun gives light to all the planets in its solar system. The light it gives to one planet doesn't lessen the light it can give to another; indeed it would be possible for it to light another ten thousand planets without its own light being dimmed. To change the picture, you can light many candles from one candle without the original losing any of its brilliance.

Jesus is a great well of blessing that constantly overflows with sheer 'grace'. If all the inhabitants of the world used enough grace to be transformed into angels, we still wouldn't have begun to diminish his endless store of grace. Why is it then, that we are so reluctant to use the grace that God has made available to us for Christian living?

Questions

1. What significance is there for us today in the fact that Jesus made a visit to this planet?
2. In what ways has John seen the 'glory' of Jesus? What does he mean by it?
3. How exactly has Jesus made God known to you? Share your story with your group, or write down your experiences.

John's gospel and the glory of Jesus

'We have seen his glory, the glory of the One and Only' (verse 14). One of the surprising things about this gospel is that it doesn't mention the transfiguration of Jesus, while the other three gospel writers do. We might have expected John to emphasize it, because he is clearly interested in the idea of glory. He uses the noun 'glory' eighteen times and the verb 'to glorify' twenty-three times (while the other gospel writers together use the noun thirteen times and the verb only nine times). These figures show that John regarded glory as an important part of the life of Christ.

Some see the transfiguration in the phrase, 'we have seen his glory' (verse 14), but John isn't saying that. If he was, he would have been more specific and referred to it directly.

Let's try and see what John means by saying, 'We have seen his glory, the glory of the One and Only' (verse 14). John's point is that we see the true glory of Jesus, not merely in the brief moment of transfiguration, but in the full thirty-three years he spent on this earth. In theological language: John sees glory in the incarnation. It was while Jesus was man that he was 'full of grace and truth' (verse 14). The wonder of the 'glory' in John's gospel is that it is a humble glory; the glory of the 'Word (become) flesh'.

Jesus' ability to reveal God

'But God the One and Only (Jesus) . . . has made him (God) known' (verse 18). If I had to write a job description for myself, I could call myself an exegete. I try to 'reveal' (*exegete*) what the

Bible says. If I'm honest, I'd have to say that I don't do it very well. But, that isn't the point. What John is saying is that Jesus 'has revealed' God; he has perfectly *'exegeted him'* is the way John puts it. Jesus is the flawless sermon about God because he is the totally accurate revelation of God.

In Rome there is a ceiling painting by Guido Reni called *The Dawn*; it depicts creation. Because it is so high up, it was very difficult to study until a mirror was placed on a table below the ceiling. Now the details of the picture can be studied in comfort and at leisure.

If we want to see what God is like, we don't need to stare into heaven. At leisure we can look down at Jesus Christ in the New Testament and see in him the perfect revelation of God. Paul said, 'In Christ all the fulness of the Deity lives in bodily form' (Colossians 2:9).

JESUS GOES PUBLIC

John 1:19–51

John 1:19–34

John the Baptist points to Jesus

John tells the Jerusalem authorities very clearly who he is and who Jesus is, and makes four great statements about the Saviour.

John confronts the authorities

Earlier in the chapter (1:6, 7 and 15), we have been told that John the Baptist's ministry was given to him by God and that it would largely consist of bearing witness to Jesus.

We now focus on John doing just that as 'the Jews of Jerusalem' send a delegation to ask him 'who he was' (verse 19). There are several code words used by John in this gospel. One that we will notice is 'the Jews'. When John says this he is invariably referring to the group of Jews opposed to Jesus. John the Baptist's ministry was highly unorthodox, so it is not surprising that the authorities wanted to question him. First, they asked him if he was 'the Christ'. He said that he wasn't, but note how he implies that the Messiah has already come (verse 26). John's strange dress probably provoked their next question: did he think he was 'Elijah' whose appearance would anticipate the end of time (Malachi 4:5)? Again John says, 'No'. Finally they ask if he was 'the prophet', a reference to the 'prophet like

Moses' who would also appear at the end of history (Deuteronomy 18:15–18).

It is only when they ask him how he would describe himself (verse 22) that John links himself with the Messiah and says that he is 'the voice of one calling in the desert, "Make straight the way for the Lord" '. The quotation is from Isaiah (40:3), who says that such a figure would announce the arrival of the Messiah.

John's witness to Jesus

John has four things to say about Jesus.

▶ *Jesus is 'the Messiah'* (1:19–28). John's focus is on Jesus; he sees himself merely as 'a voice'. But it is a voice that announces God's Anointed One, 'the Messiah'. For him, preparing the way for the Lord meant warning the people of the imminent arrival of 'the Christ'. John preached and baptized at a place where the River Jordan was shallow enough to be crossed and where, consequently, there would be plenty of coming and going, so that his message would be quickly carried across the whole country.

▶ *John saw Jesus as the 'Lamb of God'* (1:29). When the people heard John describing Jesus like this, the wealth of Old Testament teaching, which was part of their heritage, would make them think of the lamb God provided for Abraham (Genesis 22:8 and 13). Or the one whom Isaiah would describe later as being 'led like a lamb to the slaughter' (Isaiah 53:7). Or they would think of the Passover Lamb used to redeem them from slavery in Egypt (Exodus 12:3). John leaves us in no doubt as to who has provided the lamb; it was 'God's Lamb'. And the purpose of the lamb's arrival is also made clear; it was to 'take away the sin of the world'.

There is an Old Testament picture of forgiveness that we

need to rediscover today. On the Day of Atonement a goat was sacrificed to take away the sin of the people; this sin was then transferred symbolically to a second goat which was dispatched into the wilderness, never to be seen again. As the solitary animal disappeared into the distance, it was a graphic picture for the people that their 'sins' were carried away and gone for ever (Leviticus 16:21).

The New Testament suggests this same truth when John the Baptist points to Jesus and says, 'Look, the Lamb of God, who takes away the sin of the world!' The tense is the *present continuous* and speaks of our 'sin' being 'lifted up and carried away . . . lifted up and carried away'. The death of the Lamb of God acts in a present continuous way in the life of a believer. For the believer: sin *has been* dealt with, *is being* dealt with, and *will continue to be* dealt with until he or she enters heaven.

▶ *Jesus is the 'baptizer with the Spirit'* (1:32–33). We again see the marvellous humility of John the Baptist in this passage. John speaks of Jesus as the one 'the thongs of whose sandals (he is) not worthy to untie' (verse 27). The hot sun of the Middle East and the dusty unfinished roads meant that travellers arrived at their destination with very dirty, smelly feet. On arrival a host would arrange for the household slave to wash his guest's feet. There was a regulation for disciples which said, 'every service which a slave performs for his master shall a disciple do for his teacher, except the loosing of his sandal-thongs'. Surely this must have been in John's mind when he makes this statement about the sandal-thongs of Jesus. John is such a humbly committed disciple of Jesus that he counts himself 'not worthy (even to) untie' his sandals.

We don't need to ask about the ministry of John the Baptist (verse 28), his name tells us everything. John ceremonially washed people in the Jordan as a sign to mark their repentance. He 'soaked' them with water; that is what the word 'baptism' means. In the same way, says John, Jesus will 'baptise (soak) you with the Holy Spirit'. At the very least this must mean that the Messiah (the One anointed for God for this special work of redemption) has the power to anoint others in God's service.

▶ *Jesus is the 'Son of God'* (1:34). This is the name given to Jesus by God at the time of his baptism. The other gospel writers record more of what God said concerning his Son. Matthew adds, 'whom I love; with him I am well pleased' (Matthew 3:17), as does Luke (3:22).

So here are four names that are part of John's witness to Jesus: 'Messiah', 'Lamb of God', 'Baptizer with the Spirit' and 'Son of God'. In this first chapter, John actually uses eleven different names for Jesus. See if you can spot them.

Questions

1. Why does John describe Jesus as 'the Lamb of God'?
2. In what way is John the Baptist a good example for us to follow? What aspects of his lifestyle would you not follow and why?
3. What do you think John the Baptist means when he says that Jesus 'will baptise with the Holy Spirit'?

God's Christ, the Messiah

'Christ' is the Greek word which means 'anointed' and 'Messiah' is the same word in Hebrew. From the earliest times in the Old Testament, there is the idea that God will send his 'Anointed One' at some point in history to rescue and redeem his people. This teaching reaches its culmination in the prophets, particularly Isaiah who saw the Messiah as 'the suffering servant' (Isaiah 53), who 'was pierced for our transgressions', and 'was crushed for our iniquities' (Isaiah 53:5).

The first week of the new creation

We've already noticed that, by saying 'In the beginning', John caused Jewish minds to think about Genesis. There are several ideas that link John's gospel with Genesis; not least words such as 'light' and 'darkness'.

One of the features of the early chapters of Genesis is the week of creation when the solar system, and all the different parts of the animal and vegetable kingdom, were made (Genesis 1:3, 8, 13, 19, 23; 2:1 and 2:2). This is echoed in John's gospel with what we could call *a week of new creation* as Jesus begins his ministry. *Day one* is verses 19–28; we know that because verse 29 says, 'the next day'. *Day two* is verses 29–34; verse 35 says, 'the next day'. *Day three* is verses 35–42; again verse 43 says, 'the next day'. On this reckoning *Day four* must be verses 43–51. And 'on the third day' after that we have *Day seven*, when 'a wedding took place at Cana in Galilee' (2:1). John describes a complete week in the early ministry of Jesus.

John 1:35-51

Jesus starts to get his team together

In the usual Jewish way, Jesus surrounds himself
with a group of learners (disciples) and he
becomes their teacher (rabbi).

The first five disciples

The final section of this chapter begins with
John the Baptist pointing two of his own
disciples to Jesus. Once they had seen him they then 'spent the
day with him' (verse 39), and this was quickly followed by a
more committed relationship with him (verses 40–41).

This passage introduces us to the first five disciples who
decided to follow Jesus.

➤ *Andrew* (verses 40–41). Mark tells us that Andrew and Peter
   had a house in Capernaum (Mark 1:29). Both were fisher-
   men. In many ways Andrew was overshadowed by Peter
   and is even described as 'Simon Peter's brother' (1:40; 6:8).
   He couldn't hide the excitement he felt about finding Jesus
   and was soon telling his brother about it and taking him to
   Jesus. Andrew underlines the importance of telling others
   what we've found out about Jesus and simply taking them
   to the place where they can meet him for themselves.

➤ *An unnamed disciple* (verses 35–40). Sometimes it is suggested that this unnamed disciple was John, the writer of
   this gospel, but we have no way of knowing that with any
   certainty. Notice that Jesus asks these two disciples, 'What
   do you want?' (verse 38). He seems to be making sure that

they aren't just a pair of zealots who were only interested in getting rid of the Roman occupational troops.

▶ *Simon Peter* (verse 42). Straight away Jesus sees Simon's potential and gives him a new name by calling him 'a rock', which in Greek is 'Peter' and in Aramaic, 'Cephas'. (Aramaic was the local dialect of Hebrew spoken in the Palestine of New Testament times.) It took a long time for Peter to fulfil the promise foreseen by Jesus. Peter should remind us of all that we can become in Christ, even after a shaky start.

▶ *Philip* (verses 43–45). Philip is a very ordinary person who often seems to be spiritually out of his depth. In these verses it was Jesus who took the initiative and 'found' him. This seems to have happened when Jesus was in 'Galilee' (verse 43). There can be few people who won't find encouragement in the ordinariness of Philip, just as many will identify with his lack of spiritual initiative. But in spite of the absence of enterprise, he told his brother Nathanael, 'We have found the one Moses wrote about in the Law, and about whom the prophets also wrote – Jesus of Nazareth, the son of Joseph' (verse 45). Philip underlines the fact that all the Old Testament prophecies about 'the Messiah' find this fulfilment in Jesus.

▶ *Nathanael* (verses 45–51). Nathanael is not very impressed with the idea that 'the Messiah' mentioned in the Old Testament might be linked with downtown Nazareth. And he asks Philip contemptuously, 'Can anything good come from there?' It looks as if Nathanael is doing something we all do. He's thinking it highly unlikely that God would ever want to work in any place that we know – as though our knowledge of a person, place or situation limits the possibility of God working. But once Nathanael meets Jesus he discovers that there is no limit to his power: Jesus even saw him when he was sitting at home under the 'fig tree' (verse 48).

The opening remark of Jesus, 'Here is a true Israelite, in whom there is nothing false' (verse 47), might be better expressed, 'in whom there is no guile'. It is a reference to Jacob who tried to deceive his father. One translator underlines this with, 'an Israelite in whom there is no Jacob'. If Nathanael's breath was taken away by Jesus' intimate knowledge of him, he must have found the promise of the future even more astonishing.

Nathanael is mentioned in this gospel but doesn't appear in the other three. However Matthew, Mark and Luke refer to a disciple called 'Bartholomew' while John doesn't mention him at all. This has led some to believe that Nathanael and Bartholomew are the same person. This is certainly a possibility as Bartholomew is a second name meaning 'son of (Bar) Tholmai' or 'son of Ptolemy'. Such a person would need a first name and it could well have been Nathanael.

The events of Nathanael's call also tell us more about Jesus. He is 'the King of Israel' says Nathanael (verse 49). Because Jesus knew all about him, Nathanael concluded that he must be 'the Messiah' which is what he implies by calling him 'King of Israel'.

Questions

---

1. What practical lessons does John want us to learn from the examples of Andrew? Peter? Philip? Nathanael?
2. Why does Nathanael call Jesus the 'King of Israel'? Apply your answers to your personal lives, your church, your nation.
3. In what way is what Jesus says in verse 51 'an important statement'? Read Genesis 23:10–22 (especially verse 12).

How Jesus underlined what he wanted to say

Surprisingly, even today we don't have a polite way of emphasizing what we want to say; there isn't a verbal equivalent of *italics* or an *underline*. I am not thinking of shouting or jumping up and down, but some way of highlighting the words we use.

Jesus managed it; his formula was the little phrase, 'I tell you the truth' (verse 51), before an important statement, which literally means 'Amen, amen'. This is the first use of the phrase in this gospel. In future when Jesus uses it, think of him carefully *underlining* what he wants to say.

JESUS' TEACHING AND PREACHING MINISTRY

John 2:1 – 12:50

John 2:1–11

Water becomes wine

Jesus performs his first miracle ('sign') at a wedding reception, pointing to the richness of the new life.

The first 'sign'

A Jewish wedding was a once-in-a-lifetime experience. It took place in the evening: on a Wednesday if the bride was young, but on a Thursday if she was a widow. Unlike our weddings, the main figure was the bridegroom who would be expected to pay for everything. The proceedings would start when he and his friends made their way to the bride's home. As they walked they would gather other guests along the route (like the ten young ladies in Matthew 25:1–13).

For the ceremony and the celebrations afterwards, the couple would wear crowns and special robes, and be treated as royalty. Once they were married, the wedding procession would make its way to the couple's new home. As it was dark by this time the guests would hold lighted torches above their heads to illuminate the way through the streets, the bride and groom walking under a special canopy. Celebrations would then begin and last for a whole week. There was no honeymoon in the modern sense, but a wedding, especially for the poor, consisted of a few days the couple would remember for the rest of their lives.

The Jews were sticklers for tradition; it was important that everything was done properly. Drunkenness was a disgrace, but it is not too difficult to imagine the humiliation of going to the other extreme and running out of wine. There was almost a sacred obligation to provide a wedding that didn't disappoint your guests. If your neighbours had been invited to the wedding of your son, you would expect a celebration of similar quality when they returned the favour. This is probably behind the story in John 2; the bridegroom and his family were financially unable to provide the sort of wedding that was required. It is much more likely that Jesus performed a miracle to rescue the couple from a financial liability that would have crippled them for years, than to extricate them from social embarrassment.

You can look at this story as a parable of all that Jesus can do in our lives today. He can turn the ordinary (the water) into a *heady* spiritual experience (the wine). Just as when Jesus was on this earth, he was a fusion of both the divine and the human nature, so when we become Christians we are born again (see pp. 56–57) and the (divine) Holy Spirit comes to dwell in our human nature. What better way could there possibly be to describe this than to say the *water* becomes *wine*.

Questions

1. How can we be sure that Jesus wasn't like Robin Hood, a largely mythical figure? (See *A focus on Jesus* below.)
2. What 'point of need' are you aware of which you yearn for Jesus to meet? Why do you think he has not done so?
3. Why does John call the miracles of Jesus 'signs'? What exactly does this first miracle signify? (See *Miraculous signs* below.)

A focus on Jesus

John begins this chapter with a study that enables us to gauge exactly who Jesus was.

When I was very young my first hero was Robin Hood. Recently I bought a biography of him by the historian J. C. Holt. I found it disappointing because I discovered that Robin Hood wasn't a real person. The stories were probably based on Robert Hode, a highwayman convicted in Wakefield in 1225; he committed his robberies on the Great North road just north of Doncaster. There wasn't a Maid Marion, of course; she was added later to bring a touch of romance to the stories, just as Friar Tuck was intended to convey a bit of religious white-washing.

You can use the historian's principles when you open the New Testament. Notice what we discover, not that Jesus is a legend, but that he was real.

Jesus was a historical figure

'A wedding took place at Cana in Galilee' (verse 1). It was a real place, the home of the disciple Nathanael. It wasn't a made-up name like *Ambridge*. We may not like what Jesus said, or want what he offers, but you can't say that he didn't actually live in Palestine at a certain time in history and make offers to those who followed him.

Jesus was a divine figure

'The water . . . had been turned into wine' (verse 9). Throughout the gospels we see the divinity of Jesus in his ability to work miracles. They were clearly 'miraculous signs' (verse 11) and impossible to explain away. On this occasion we are talking about 'twenty to thirty gallons' (verse 6) of water being turned into the equivalent of 500–800 bottles of wine, of the standard size you would find on the shelf in your local supermarket. We don't know about the other guests, but for the disciples this miracle showed them the 'glory' (verse 11) of Jesus.

Jesus was a human figure

Judea was part of the Roman Empire and consequently had an occupying army. The Jewish leaders longed for the Messiah to come to free them from the power of Rome and rid the country of foreign soldiers. The leaders would have had no problem with the idea that the Messiah was *divine* but to suggest that he might also be *human* presented them with difficulties.

Had they stopped to think, they would have realized that the humanness of Jesus actually made him able to 'sympathise with (their) weaknesses' and therefore they would be able to 'receive mercy and find grace to help . . . in (their) time of need' (Hebrews 4:15–16).

Sometimes people feel that Jesus wasn't a very caring son to address his mother as 'dear woman' (verse 4). In the older translations he just says 'woman'; but the word, far from being abrupt or neglectful, is actually an expression of courtesy and respect.

Jesus was an authoritative figure

'When the wine was gone, Jesus' mother said to him, "They have no more wine"' (verse 3). In western culture today it is the bride's father who pays for the reception and as we've already seen in the Judea of Jesus' day it was the groom. But Jesus fills neither of these positions. So we need to ask, 'Why is Jesus being told that the wine has run out?' The answer is that he is an authoritative figure. It is a universal truth that runs through the gospels; if a man is blind it is to Jesus that he comes for help; if a woman is 'subject to bleeding for twelve years' it is the edge of his cloak that she wants to touch.

Jesus was a relevant figure

The heading for the first paragraph of chapter two is, 'Jesus changes water to wine' and that sums it up exactly. Notice Jesus didn't offer to give them the latest book, or video, or even offer someone to counsel them. He meets them at their point of need; this is something that happens right through the gospels.

Miraculous signs

'This, the first of his miraculous signs' (verse 11). 'Sign' is one of the ways John refers to miracles. He doesn't call them 'mighty works' as the other gospel writers do. To call them a 'sign' tells us that they convey spiritual truth and meaning. The other word John uses for miracle is 'work' (4:34). The word is interesting because John uses it for both the miraculous and the non-miraculous things Jesus did. By this he clearly implies that for Jesus there wasn't much difference between the two; he is Lord of both the natural and the supernatural world.

John 2:12–25

Jesus clears out the temple

Jesus visits the temple in Jerusalem at the
time of a major religious festival and is
offended by the proceedings of the
'church of the day'.

The Passover

The Jews had three major festivals in their
calendar of which 'the Passover' (verse 13)
was one. Every adult male Jew living within a fifteen-mile radius
of Jerusalem had to attend (Deuteronomy 16:16). And it was the
dream of every Jew scattered across the ancient world that at one
'Passover' they would return to Jerusalem to celebrate the feast
at the heart of Judaism. 'Passover' fell on the 15th Nisan, about
the middle of our April.

In the Old Testament 'Passover' meant 'to spare'. The festival
commemorated the night when the first-born of the Jewish
slaves were spared death as the nation escaped from Egypt. The
door-frame of their houses had to be painted with the blood of a
lamb; the lamb itself was enjoyed by the family at a special
meal.

In the time of Jesus the people would gather in the outer court
of the temple to witness the slaughter of the paschal lambs. The
priests stood in two rows. The front row would hold a gold basin
and the back row a silver one. These basins were used to catch
the blood of the expiring lambs and were passed in a continuous
movement along the line of priests. The last one would throw the
blood over the altar.

The new broom sweeps clean

This section shows us the relationship between Jesus and the established religion of his day.

He was angry at the impression the temple gave to the outside world

'In the temple courts he found men selling cattle, sheep and doves, and others sitting at tables exchanging money' (verse 14). All this trading was done in the Court of the Gentiles and had been allowed since the time when Annas was High Priest and consequently it was known as the Bazaar of Annas.

The money changers were needed because the offerings had to be given in Tyrian coinage, which was the only approved currency. The Tyrians were a trading nation and knew the benefits of a stable and accurate currency. Their coins were always the right weight and contained the right amount of precious metal.

Besides the money changers there were stalls that sold oxen, sheep and doves for the various sacrifices. You could bring your own animal, but it would need to be inspected by the temple authorities for a fee. And it would be more than likely that such animals would be rejected on some pretence or another, so you would be forced to buy one from an official stall in the temple. 'So (Jesus) made a whip out of cords, and drove all from the temple area, both sheep and cattle; he scattered the coins of the money changers' (verse 15).

The nearest that the Gentiles would get to the sanctuary was the Bazaar of Annas. So instead of seeing the 'Father's house' all they would see would be a 'market' (verse 16).

Jesus foresees his resurrection

'Get these out of here! How dare you turn my Father's house into a market!' (verse 16). This is not merely the action of a zealous social reformer; it is a claim to be the Messiah. The Jews recognized this. 'What miraculous sign can you show us to prove your authority to do all this?' (verse 18). Jesus normally refused to give signs, but occasionally he points to the resurrection and that is what he does here. 'Destroy this temple, and I will raise it again in three days' (verse 19). The Jews did not understand that he was referring to his own body, but all this encouraged the disciples, especially after Jesus' death and resurrection. 'Then they believed the Scripture and the words that Jesus had spoken' (verse 22).

Questions

1. How far do special places help you in your personal prayer (e.g. a church building, a quiet corner, a superb view)? Share your experiences with the group.
2. What equivalents to the traders in the temple do you see in today's church? (Do not get stuck with charging for entrance to cathedrals!)
3. Does the church today represent Jesus in his resurrection authority (verse 18–19)? If so, what money-changers' tables ought we to be upsetting in the world around us?

The temple courts

It was Herod's temple that Jesus visited when he 'went up to Jerusalem' (verse 14). Herod began building in 19 BC and although the main structure was completed within a decade (c. 9 BC), work continued off and on until AD 64.

From hindsight it is obvious that Herod didn't build the temple to glorify God, but rather to placate the Jewish people and make them more willing to put up with him (he was not a Jew himself but an Idumean).

The building consisted of a series of rectangular courts within each other. The large outside rectangle was the Court of the Gentiles, which measured some 450 metres by 250 metres. Within this court was a low wall with openings in it; only those with Jewish blood could enter beyond this barrier and any non-Jew entered on pain of death. Once within the wall there was another rectangle; this was the Court of the Women which enclosed the Court of Israel, and the Court of the Priests which was the innermost sanctuary. Each court was more exclusive than the last.

John 3:1–15

Jesus and Nicodemus

Jesus talks to Nicodemus about being 'born from above', the vital key to entry into his kingdom.

Nicodemus

His name

'Nicodemus' was a Greek name which suggests that he originally came from a Jewish family who lived somewhere in the eastern part of the Roman Empire, where Greek was spoken. It is possible that the family had made enough money to return to Jerusalem and wanted to get involved in politics. Someone called Nicodemus survived the destruction of Jerusalem by the Romans in AD 70; it could easily have been this man.

His theological position

He was a 'Pharisee' (verse 1). Just as some of us have different theological labels (e.g. 'charismatic' or 'reformed'), so did the Jews in Bible times. It wouldn't be too far wrong to suggest that the Sadducees were the liberals; they rejected the idea of resurrection, angels and demons. Most priests were Sadducees. Today we might describe the Pharisees as 'extreme conservatives'. In the days of Nicodemus there were about 6,000 of them. 'Pharisee' meant 'separated one' and when the movement began in about 135 BC, it was a campaign of great vision to separate people to God. But very quickly it degenerated into an exclusive movement to separate Pharisees from ordinary people. In their arrogance they said, 'the crowd who knows not the law is accursed'.

Probably the key verses about the Pharisees in the New Testament are: 'Everything they do is done for men to see: They make their phylacteries wide and the tassels on their garments long; they love the place of honour at banquets and the most important seats in the synagogues' (Matthew 23:5–6). For those of us who are Bible-believing Christians it is a healthy reminder not to fall to the temptation of outward show of religion at the expense of inner holiness of life.

His job

'Nicodemus, a member of the Jewish ruling council' (verse 1). He was a member of the Sanhedrin, the Parliament of the Jewish people and would be the equivalent of an English MP or an American senator.

Family background

Later, we are told that Nicodemus 'brought a mixture of myrrh and aloes, about seventy-five pounds (weight)' to prepare the body of Jesus for burial (19:39). This suggests that he came from a very wealthy family.

A profile of his character

'He came to Jesus at night' (verse 2). This seems to imply that he was a shy, timid, person who didn't want to be too conspicuous. In other words, he was just like many ordinary people today. He feared that his reputation might be compromised by being seen with a religious figure.

The choice we have to make

Notice, 'I tell you the truth' (verses 3, 5 and 11), the formula which announces that Jesus is about to say something significant. It comes three times, so this conversation must contain some weighty themes that we need to notice. Indeed Jesus does speak about three important matters, but before we look at these, note that Nicodemus doesn't appear to understand him: 'How can a man . . .?' (verse 4); 'How can this be?' (verse 9). One reason for this response could be that Nicodemus didn't like what was said. We react in the same way when we say, 'I don't know what you're talking about?' in response to someone pointing at things in our lives that we are not ready to talk about.

Questions

___

1. What Pharisee-like 'externals' are you in danger of getting caught up with? How can this be avoided?
2. What do you understand by the phrase 'kingdom of God'? To what extent is your life part of it?
3. Why is it essential to be 'born again'? What does it mean?
4. What does 'eternal life' mean? What do we have to do to get it? Why?

The kingdom of God

'The kingdom of God' (verse 5) is the most frequent topic of Jesus' teaching in the other gospels, but is quite rare in John's gospel. It is not to be understood geographically, but dynamically. That is, it is the place where God reigns; it is not a country where he rules. Wherever he 'reigns', whether it is in heaven or in a believer's life, that is 'the kingdom of God'.

Born again

'Unless (a man) is born again' (verse 3); the adverb has several meanings. It can simply mean 'again' in the sense of 'one more time'; or 'from the beginning' or 'from the top'. Note, elsewhere in the New Testament, some uses of the word translated 'again'. For example, in Luke's account of the life of Jesus he says that he had 'carefully investigated everything from the *beginning*' (Luke 1:3). Mark tells us that when Jesus died, 'the curtain of the temple was torn in two from *top* to bottom' (Mark 15:38). And later in this gospel John describes how, at the time of the death of Christ, the soldiers took his robe and that it 'was seamless, woven in one piece from *top* to bottom' (19:23). We won't be far amiss if we say that to be 'born again' means to 'be reborn from above'.

The emphasis that rebirth relates to the spiritual life comes several times. Man must be 'born of water and the Spirit' (verse 5); there is no natural progression from one birth to the next. Notice too that 'the wind blows wherever it pleases' (verse 8). Even today, with weather satellites 22,000 miles above the earth, we still can't predict exactly which way the wind will blow; so the work of the Holy Spirit is not within our control or knowing. The spiritual nature of the 'new birth' is again highlighted by the distinction made between 'earthly things' and 'heavenly things' (verse 12).

When we are 'born from above' ('regeneration' is another way the Bible describes this work) the Holy Spirit's work is sovereign. But there is no way that God will invade our lives unless invited to do so. The evidence is that Nicodemus was 'born again', so at some time he must have asked God's forgiveness and invited him into his life to make him regenerate. We will need to do the same if we want to be 'born again' and enjoy 'eternal life' (verse 15).

Eternal life

If you were to ask people today about 'eternal life' (verse 15), most people would probably say that it refers to the life that begins when we get to heaven and which will last for ever. The implication being that in twentieth-century English 'eternal life' speaks about something that is everlasting. But that is not what Jesus is saying; it is not its duration that he has in mind, but its quality. 'Eternal life' is the 'life of God's age'; and it is the essential intensity of that life that Jesus is talking about. One writer goes as far as saying it is 'resurrection life' and that is a good description. Elsewhere, in the older translations, Jesus speaks about 'abundant life' (John 10:10 AV); that is it exactly. Of course, once we get to heaven 'eternal life' will last for ever, but that is not the emphasis here.

Jesus explains how this 'life' can be enjoyed. He reminds Nicodemus of the story in Numbers 21 where venomous snakes had bitten the Israelites. As the bite was fatal, Moses prayed and the remedy God revealed was that the people were to make a bronze snake and put it up on a pole where everybody could see it. Whoever looked at the snake would live.

In exactly the same way Jesus says he is to be 'lifted up' (verse 14). He doesn't actually mention the cross here, but it must have been in his mind. As the Israelites looked at the bronze snake to be healed so we need to look at Christ and 'believe in him' to be saved and have 'eternal life' (verse 15).

John 3:16–21

The gospel in miniature

The writer reflects on what Jesus has been saying and gives us a summary of the best of all good news.

All agree that, from time to time, John meditates on what has been said. But because there were no quotation marks in the first century, it is sometimes difficult to be precise  about where Jesus stops speaking and John starts reflecting. In the passage we've just looked at, Jesus starts to reply in verse 10 and he appears to be still speaking in verse 15, because 'Son of Man' (verse 15) is a way that he often refers to himself. So we may presume that John starts to ruminate in verse sixteen.

God's love

We now come to probably the best known text in the Bible. But our familiarity with it can mask the astonishing impact it must have made on the early church. From the Old Testament they knew that God loved his people and that he loved sinners. So note that we're now told that he 'loved the world' (verse 16). To the original readers of this gospel, that must have stood out like a neon-sign on a dark road. Martin Luther called this verse *the gospel in miniature*, because it contains everything we need to know for salvation.

God's gift

God not only 'loved the world' (verse 16), he also 'gave' it a gift. The construction of the phrase emphasizes the gift, 'he gave his one and only Son'. One commentator points out that John, more than any other writer, reports Jesus as characterizing the Father as *'the-having-sent-me-Father'*, which is true; it is an expression that he uses several times.

God's purpose

John concludes this contemplation by noting that 'God's love' focused on 'the gift', which in turn highlighted the purpose. He 'did not send his Son into the world to condemn the world, but to save the world through him' (verse 17). So we are presented with two stark alternatives: to 'perish' or to have 'eternal life'. And we move from one to the other by 'believing'. Indeed anyone who 'does not believe stands condemned already' (verse 18).

Accepting God's gift

Imagine at this point you say to yourself, 'I don't think I am ready yet to make that leap of faith and become a Christian.' My answer would be that there is no foundation for such a statement. In the Bible, and in life for that matter, faith has three component parts: (i) *knowledge*, (ii) *belief* and (iii) *trust*. In the next chapter we will see Jesus heal an official's son (p. 73). When the man came to see Jesus he already had some *knowledge* about him and his ability to heal his son who 'was close to death' (verse 47). He *believed* what Jesus had said (verse 49) and finally *trusted* him when he said, 'Your son will live' (verse 50).

Let's look at faith operating in a non-biblical situation. Imagine that you are away from home and feeling hungry. You spot a Pizzeria and know that they are in the business of providing food; here is knowledge. You find a table and look at the menu. When the waitress arrives, you order a Pizza Pavarotti believing what the menu offers; here is *belief*. You then sit trusting that it will arrive.

In exactly the same way, when you make the step of faith to become a Christian it starts with knowledge, the sort of knowledge that John has already given us in this gospel. When you are ready there will come a time when you can say, 'Yes, I believe this'. Faith is never a 'leap in the dark'; it is always a response to the facts that we have been given. The evidence is that Nicodemus believed and trusted the facts (the knowledge that Jesus had provided) and we can do the same.

Questions

1. What is 'astonishing' about the impact which verse 16 would have made on the early church?
2. Why do those who don't believe 'stand condemned already'?
3. In your group take it in turns to play the role of someone who says 'I'd like to believe but I can't'. Group members take turns to be 'counsellors' (don't all descend at once on the 'non-believer'!).

John 3:22–35

The testimony of John the Baptist

John resists the temptation to rival Jesus and humbly points his followers to 'one greater than I'.

 The scene now moves to 'the Judean country-side' (verse 22), and not far away at 'Aenon near Salim' (verse 23) John the Baptist was at work. The Dead Sea Scrolls have shown that there was a great deal of interest in ceremonial washing at this time. John's title reveals that he emphasized the rite of 'ceremonial washing' (verse 25).

Since the church still differs over 'baptism' it is not surprising that a dispute arose between 'John's disciples and a certain Jew over the matter' (verse 25). It may be worth noting that the dispute was between John's disciples and someone else, while John, the leader of the group, just got on with his task.

John defuses any sense of rivalry

At this point John's star is waning and the new person to hear was definitely Jesus. He was now so popular that it felt as if 'everybody (was) going to him' (verse 26). Some of John's disciples still felt that John was the greater prophet; so they saw Jesus as a rival and a threat.

A sense of rivalry between ministries is a not very subtle way of hindering the gospel. It doesn't matter who we are, or how great a success we've made of Sunday School teaching or preaching or the house group, one day someone is going to come along who will be the next leader. Note that there is no sense of bitterness in John that someone new has appeared.

John's simple philosophy

John turns to his followers and they are gently rebuked: 'A man can receive only what is given him from heaven' (verse 27). That simple statement puts John in the world class of leaders; it is, therefore, no wonder that Jesus said, 'I tell you the truth: Among those born of women there has not risen anyone greater than John the Baptist' (Matthew 11:11). The way we imagine ourselves to be special people because of the gifts that God has chosen to give us makes no sense at all. John the Baptist was special because he recognized the source of all gifts.

John's understanding of his role

There is no doubt in John's mind about Jesus. 'I am not the Christ but am sent ahead of him' (verse 28). But John now realizes that his ministry of preparation is over. That Jesus 'the bridegroom' (verse 29) has come for his 'bride' and he sees himself as no more than the groom's 'friend'. But his joy is 'complete' because the time of waiting is over; God's Christ has come. As John looks at Jesus, there is only one thing he can say, 'He must become greater; I must become less'.

This principle applies to us too and some suggest that we need to pretend to be worthless. But I don't think it is necessary to belittle ourselves, or anything that we do. But, rather like Mary, we must learn to 'magnify the Lord' (Luke 1:46, AV). If we do this to other people as well, then we will have what Paul describes as the mind of Christ (Philippians 2:2), so others will become greater and we less.

Questions

1. Are you aware of any sense of rivalry between ministries in which you are involved? Why is this so damaging? How can it be dealt with?

2. What made John the Baptist really special? What can we learn from him?
3. What parallels are there between Christian ministry and the role of the 'bridegroom's friend' in first-century Palestine? (See below.)

'The bridegroom's friend': a pattern for ministry

'The friend who attends the bridegroom' (verse 29). Hidden in that phrase is a whole new concept of ministry. 'The friend' is the equivalent of our 'best man', but in a Jewish wedding he fulfilled a much more important place. He arranged the wedding; and took out the invitations. He brought the bride and the groom together and presided at the wedding feast. And when it was all over, he still had one last special duty which was to guard the bridal chamber and bar the way to any false lover. When he heard the groom's voice and recognized it, he let him in. He could then rejoice that his task was over; he had fulfilled his job.

There can be no greater view of ministry than to consider ourselves to be the 'bridegroom's friend'.

The bride

The prophets in the Old Testament often used the idea of Israel and God being like a 'bride and groom' (Isaiah 62:5; 54:5; Hosea 2:19–20; Ezekiel 16). Jesus identifies himself with the 'bride-groom' in some of the parables (Matthew 9:14–15; 22:1–14; 25:1–13). John the Baptist uses the picture here. And Paul develops the idea to describe his ministry as preparing the church for the final espousal when Jesus returns (2 Corinthians 11:2). He sees marriage as the true analogy of the relationship between Jesus and the church (Ephesians 5:22–32).

John 4:1–15

The woman at the well

Jesus talks to a Samaritan woman about 'living water' and points her towards spiritual life.

The way to the well (verses 1–7)

Everything had gone well for Jesus and his team of disciples and then suddenly their work was overshadowed by a rumour. The Pharisees 'heard that Jesus was gaining and baptising more disciples than John' (verse 1). When Jesus heard this, he 'left Judea and went back once more to Galilee' (verse 2). He seemed to have realized the cancerous nature of this bit of gossip, and he knew how the Pharisees would twist it until the people believed that he and John were in opposition. Even though the remark was untrue the damage had been done, and there was no point in lingering another day. So he left the crowd to John the Baptist, hoping that if he got away quickly, the blessing would continue in Judea.

Imagine three square building bricks belonging to a child. Place them vertically one on top of the other. What you will see is the geography of first-century Palestine. The bottom brick would be Judea, the top one Galilee and the one sandwiched in the middle, Samaria. Jesus took the obvious route from Judea to

Galilee which was to travel straight 'through Samaria' (verse 4). Most Jews would not travel that way. They would studiously miss Samaria by travelling east, crossing the Jordan into Perea, then heading north to Decapolis and only then turn west into Galilee.

The strained relationship between the two communities went back at least 700 years. In 721 BC the Assyrians had swept through the Northern Kingdom and taken the inhabitants into captivity. Once there, the Jews intermarried with the Assyrians and, when they returned, they became known as 'Samaritans'. In 587 BC the Babylonians took the Jews from the Southern Kingdom into captivity, but they refused to intermarry with the Babylonians. And when they returned to their land, they claimed to have pure Jewish blood, because they hadn't intermarried. An implacable hatred developed between the two groups; the Jews and the Samaritans.

'Jacob's Well' (verse 6) was at a fork in the road near a town 'called Sychar' (verse 4). The well and the land around it are both mentioned in the Old Testament (Genesis 33:18–19; Joshua 24:32). A 'well' is normally a vertical shaft sunk into the ground to obtain water; the word here means 'spring or fountain', implying that this particular well was supplied by a spring.

The woman at the well (verses 8–9)

Jesus was tired and he was resting by the well at midday (verse 6 'sixth hour'). The 'disciples had gone into the town to buy food' when 'a Samaritan woman came to draw water'.

There is much in this story that would have staggered the Jews of Jesus' day and shown them that Jesus was not bound by their prejudices.

▶ She is a woman and rabbis didn't normally talk to women.

▶ What's more, she is a Samaritan woman.

▶ Jesus asks for a drink, which would technically be 'unclean' if she drew the water.

▶ He goes on to have a lengthy spiritual discussion with her. Rabbi Eliezer said, 'If a man gives his daughter a knowledge of the law it is as though he taught her lechery'.

Jesus points to 'the gift of God'. He doesn't explain what this was, but presumably he was referring to 'living water' (verse 10).

The living water that leaps (verses 10–15)

To our ears, 'living water' sounds like the fabulous water of a fairy tale, but to the inhabitants of first-century Palestine it meant 'fresh' or 'running water', water that wasn't stagnant. But Jesus obviously meant something much more than that. Later he spoke of 'living water' flowing from the believer who had experienced the Holy Spirit through him (7:38). But the Samaritan woman wasn't ready to think about spiritual matters and pointed out that Jesus didn't even have a bucket to use to draw the water. Or, she queried, was he suggesting that he didn't need a container and was, therefore, 'greater than our father Jacob' who had drawn water in the normal way?

You would think that the woman's inability to see beyond ordinary water would be shattered when Jesus said, 'Everyone who drinks this water will be thirsty again, but whoever drinks the water I give him will never thirst. Indeed, the water I give him will become in him a spring of water welling up to eternal life' (verses 13–14). Literally this means the water that 'leaps' up to eternal life. The translators have used the phrase 'wells up' because the verb wasn't normally used of inanimate things like water; it was more commonly used of people or animals that 'jumped up into the air'. But Jesus is not talking of a natural force and certainly not an inanimate one! When the Holy Spirit becomes part of our lives, he is a vital force who will find vigorous expression.

Questions

1. In what ways can gossip be cancerous? Discuss situations where this has happened (but avoid gossip!).
2. What features of this account would have staggered the Jews of Jesus' day? What does this tell us about Jesus?
3. Why is the imagery of 'living water' such a good way of describing the Holy Spirit?
4. Jesus was a Jew. How far should Christians of all nationalities worship a *Jewish* saviour? Should we think of him purely as 'one of us'?

John 4:16–30

Worship in spirit and in truth

Jesus skilfully leads the conversation from water supply to spiritual worship and from outward forms of worship to encounter with the truth.

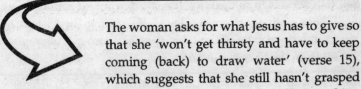

The woman asks for what Jesus has to give so that she 'won't get thirsty and have to keep coming (back) to draw water' (verse 15), which suggests that she still hasn't grasped what Jesus was talking about. She simply wants to humour him. But with his intimate knowledge of her personal life, it slowly begins to dawn on her and she becomes more attentive and serious. Again there are several things we need to notice:

▶ 'Our fathers worshipped on this mountain' (verse 20). The

antagonism between the Jews and the Samaritans spilled over to many subjects and the proper place of worship was one of the most notable. The Jews believed that it should be in Jerusalem and so had built the temple there. The Samaritans, however, held that Mount Gerizim was the right place. They said that was the place where God had blessed people (Deuteronomy 11:29; 27:12) and that he had commanded that an altar should be built (Deuteronomy 27:4–5). Our Bibles tell us that the altar was built on Mount Ebal, but the Samaritan scriptures read Mount Gerizim at this point.

▶ 'You Samaritans worship what you do not know' (verse 22). Jesus points to the gap in the spiritual knowledge of the Samaritans which sprang mostly from their refusal to have any Scripture other than the first five books of the Old Testament. Disregarding the rest of the Old Testament meant that they had little or no understanding of how God had looked after his people down the centuries.

▶ 'You . . . worship what . . .' (verse 22). Jesus doesn't say 'who'. There is no doubt that the Samaritans worshipped the true God, but in rejecting much of his revelation, their system of worship lacked a vital element – personal relationship with God.

▶ 'Salvation is from the Jews' (verse 22). The text actually says, '*The* salvation is from the Jews'. By cutting themselves off from a good part of the Bible they had also cut themselves off from the way of salvation.

▶ 'Worship the Father in spirit and truth' (verse 23). This is a development of the same point. 'Truth' is what God has revealed; to remove part of that revelation means we haven't got the whole 'truth' and, therefore, any subsequent behaviour can't be in the 'spirit' of that truth.

▶ 'God is spirit' (verse 24). By ascribing spirituality to God we are saying that he has none of the properties that belong to *matter* and that he cannot be discerned by bodily senses. Being 'spirit' does not mean we should think of him as 'a gas' or 'an energy force', because these things still have physical dimensions. The best analogy to *spirit* is *mind*. The mind is distinct from the brain. It has no physical dimension, it is spiritual. God, as spirit, can be everywhere at once, eternal and infinite. 'Must worship . . .' It is not simply a good idea to worship God; it is an imperative, something that we 'must' do.

▶ '(The) Messiah', 'I . . . am he' (verses 25–26). The woman knew that the 'Messiah (the Christ) is coming'. And Jesus replied (literally), 'I who speak to you, I am'. Both partners in the conversation are now speaking and understanding on the same level.

Questions

1. Why was Samaritan worship inevitably flawed? How do you think this might be relevant for us today? How can we grasp what the whole Bible is telling us?
2. What do we mean when we say that 'God is spirit'?
3. Why is worshipping God something that we *must* do? Does this apply only to Christians who choose to worship or to the whole human race?

A model of how to speak to people about important things

Notice that from the beginning of the conversation the other person is involved. The fact that she is a Samaritan and Jesus is a

Jew means that she queries his request, giving him the opportunity to speak about spiritual things. This is excellent inductive teaching. Nothing is forced; Jesus is not rude, there is no hint of chauvinism or racism, yet somehow he gets to the heart of the matter very quickly. Once it is obvious that she is interested, notice how quickly Jesus moves on to moral issues and reveals that he knows just how unfaithful and promiscuous she has been. Of course if we are to speak to people about spiritual matters, our lives must reflect what we say. *Belief* and *behaviour* always go hand in hand; one must always reflect the other. We live in a society that lacks sexual restraint, but if what John is writing about is beginning to make sense, then it must be reflected in our behaviour. There is no way that a believer can ever be free to sleep around. If Jesus is changing our thinking, we must start to 'walk' in his ways too.

John 4:31-54

Harvest and healing

Jesus once more points away from the physical (food) to the spiritual ('fruit for eternal life') and performs a healing miracle as a sign of new life.

Fields ready for harvest (verses 31-38)

Between 'Jacob's well' at the foot of Mount
Gerizim and the village of Aschar at the foot
of Mount Ebal was the plain of Mukhna, used for growing wheat. When the 'disciples returned' from the village with food they found Jesus 'talking with a woman' (verse 27). The

'disciples urged him, "Rabbi, eat something".' Jesus replied, 'My food is to do the will of him who sent me'.

Doing God's will

It was meat and drink for Jesus 'to do the will of him who' had sent him (verse 34). That was his reason for coming to the earth, and therefore it was more important for him than the food the disciples had just brought back from the village. 'Him who sent me' is a distinctive way that John has of referring to the mission of Jesus. 'To do the will' of God was not a matter of an occasional impulse; Jesus carried it right through to the conclusion, until it was 'finished'.

The harvest that is ready

The conversation that Jesus had with the disciples is similar to the one with the Samaritan woman; he is talking about one thing and they were hearing something else. The key is his mission and his desire to get on with it. Maybe Jesus was still resting on the well and the disciples had their back to the plain of Mukhna where the first green shoots of corn had appeared. He quotes a proverb to them, 'Do you not say, "Four months more and then the harvest"? . . . open your eyes and look at the fields!' (verse 35). The words of a recent traveller describe something Jesus might have been watching as he spoke to the disciples: 'As I sat by Jacob's well a crowd of Arabs came along the road from the direction in which Jesus was looking, and I saw their white garments shining in the sun.' With his mission in mind, what Jesus probably saw was a small group of Samaritans coming out from the village to hear him. It was human beings who were 'fields . . . ripe for harvest'.

In our world of city-dwellers and technology, agricultural images are not always obvious. But the Old Testament is full of metaphors taken from country life. Today, God is still looking for a people who know him and who reflect this in the way they live. The Bible calls such a people 'the garden of his delight' (Isaiah 5:7). Jesus calls them a 'crop for eternal life' (verse 36).

New life in Samaria and Galilee (verses 39–54)

Many Samaritans believe

Jesus was very patient with this woman. And having come to faith she immediately leaves her water jar and returns to the village to share what she has discovered; with the result that 'Many of the Samaritans from that town believed in' Jesus (verse 39). And when they actually heard him for themselves, 'many more became believers' and said 'this man really is the Saviour of the world'.

Galileans welcome Jesus

The action now moves to Galilee and we notice two things.

1. Jesus says, 'A prophet has no honour in his own country' (verse 44) which seems to refer to Galilee. But, in spite of this proverb:
2. 'The Galileans welcomed him' (verse 45). Their ground for doing so was that 'they had seen all that he had done in Jerusalem at the Passover Feast'. However, their enthusiasm seems to have been related to 'signs and wonders' rather than a conviction that he was the 'Christ' and the 'Saviour of the world'.

A certain royal official

John's description of the man as a 'certain royal official' points to him being in the service of Herod (Antipas). Strictly speaking Herod wasn't a king, but a 'tetrarch', or 'a ruler of a fourth part'. The Romans used the word indiscriminately for regional rulers. When Herod (the Great) died, his territory was divided among his three sons and Herod (Antipas) got Galilee and Perea. Herod no doubt, remembered that his father called himself king and so occasionally used the title himself. The father involved here was probably an official working for Herod the tetrarch. He lived at Capernaum, some twenty miles from Cana (verse 46).

Signs and wonders

Verse 48 is a reminder that in every age people have been attracted to the spectacular. But to get caught up with 'signs' and miss what they are pointing to is a tragedy; similarly to marvel at a 'wonder' and miss what God has done is sad. As always, Jesus is concerned that in spite of seeing 'signs and wonders' the people do not believe; the spectacular had fed their curiosity, but not their commitment.

The road to faith

Although he didn't know the healer's name, or have faith, the father's desperation made him plead for his son's life. The reply of Jesus was unexpected, 'You may go. Your son will live' (verse 50). Presumably he hoped Jesus would return with him and that they would both get there in time. The possibility of Jesus healing at a distance hadn't occurred to him. Now he seemed to have faith and he 'took Jesus at his word and departed' for Capernaum. His reward was to discover later that his son was cured at the exact moment when Jesus pronounced his words of healing. Now the spectacular is not merely a matter of curiosity, but conviction. 'So he and all his household believed' (verse 53).

Questions

1. How can doing God's will be regarded as 'food'? To what extent would you say this is true for you? Do you often feel hungry?
2. What lies behind the apparent contradiction between verses 44 and 45? What practical differences are there between 'welcoming' and 'honouring' Jesus? How far does your church encourage both?
3. What does the story of the healing of the official's son teach us about the meaning of true faith?

John 5:1–15

The healing at the pool

Jesus heals a man who has been an invalid for thirty-eight years. But the healing is on the Sabbath and this sparks a row with the Jewish leaders.

'Some time later' Jesus went up to Jerusalem at the time of 'a feast of the Jews' (verse 1). It is impossible to identify which feast John had in mind; some think it was Pentecost, coming

fifty days after Passover (John 2:13), while others speculate that it might have been Tabernacles. It doesn't actually matter; John is simply telling us that Jerusalem would be full of visitors because of a feast.

The pool (verses 1–2)

A much more fascinating conundrum has to do with the pool. The original text is slightly mysterious, 'Now there is in Jerusalem near the Sheep . . .' (verse 2), but Sheep *what* we're not told. Most modern scholars think that John was referring to the 'Sheep Gate', but the older translators are inclined to think that it was the 'Sheep Market' (AV). One notable modern scholar thinks it should be 'Sheep Pool', which is the suggestion favoured by most of the ancient writers and teachers. As you will see in a moment, this seems to have been confirmed by the Dead Sea Scrolls.

Another difficulty arises, not from what John has left out, but from the name that the scribes, who copied the scrolls, have put in. The best supported name is 'Bethsaida' (meaning House of Fish, or House of the Fisher). Other manuscripts call the pool

'Bethzatha', 'Bezetha' or 'Belzetha', while the NIV and the AV have 'Bethesda' (meaning House of Mercy).

The Dead Sea Scrolls refer to a number of places around Jerusalem, one of which was 'Beth Eshdatain'. Names in both Hebrew and Aramaic, in addition to being singular and plural, also have a 'dual' form. And 'Beth Eshdatain' is a dual noun, implying that there were two of them. Archaeologists have found a double pool which today is known as St Anne's Pool; there seems little doubt that this was where the miracle took place. Therefore we read, 'In Jerusalem near the Sheep Pool was a pool which in Aramaic is called Bethesda . . .' This had 'five colonnades', four around the sides and one between the two pools.

The crowd (verses 3–6)

The colonnades were crowded with people suffering from a variety of illnesses. They were waiting for the water to be 'stirred' as that seemed the most propitious moment for healing. There are two possible explanations behind the disturbance of the water.

1. The *supply came from elsewhere*, perhaps from the temple, so that when the source was turned on there would have been a rippling effect on the surface.
2. The pool was a *thermal spring* which bubbled up from time to time.

The latter seems the most likely explanation, because there are thermal pools in the world today which give a similar hope of healing for sufferers: Lourdes in France and Guadalupe in Mexico are the most notable.

The healing (verses 5–15)

We are not told exactly what caused the man's condition; verse 8 seems to suggest that he was lame. What we do know is that he had been like that for thirty-eight years. When Jesus learned this, he asked the man, 'Do you want to get well?' It isn't such a surprising question because someone who has been ill for that amount of time would have developed a pattern and a rhythm of living that enabled him to cope. The man would know what he could manage to do and what he couldn't; and those who wanted to help him would know where to find him. But once he was healed everything would change. Jesus was asking him if he was prepared for that. In exactly the same way the imagery here applies to us. Do we really want to be forgiven? Are we prepared for the changes that conversion will inevitably bring?

This man was only able to think about healing in terms of the water being agitated and the fact that he couldn't get into it without help. On the other hand Jesus doesn't hesitate. 'Get up! Pick up your mat and walk' (verse 8). The cure was immediate. As with all the miracles of Jesus the healing was unquestionably supernatural; there were no physiotherapists to tone up his muscles for their unaccustomed task and limbs that hadn't been used for thirty-eight years functioned immediately. 'At once . . . he picked up his mat and walked' (verse 9).

It wasn't me!

The healed man was interrogated by the leaders. There can be little doubt that he knew the Sabbath regulations, because everybody did. The rules allowed an invalid to be carried on his mat; 'he is not culpable by reason of the mat, since the mat is secondary' (*Shabbath* 10:5). But the healing changed everything; now the mat ceased to be his bed and became an object to be carried. And that was not allowed.

'Stop sinning' (verses 13–14)

The man wasn't a follower of Jesus; he hadn't been healed because of his faith. Jesus simply had compassion on him. So when he met him later in the temple Jesus said, 'See, you are well again. Stop sinning' (verse 14). It begs the fascinating question as to whether the man had gone to the temple to give thanks.

Questions

---

1. At first sight, Jesus' question to the man in verse 6 seems rather odd. How can we account for it? How would it apply to the offer of new Christian life to an unbeliever?
2. What relationship between sickness and sin is implied by this passage? Do you think that this always applies? Why/why not?
3. Is faith always necessary for healing? What value is there in pilgrimages to Lourdes and other such centres?

The minefield of Sabbath do's and don'ts (verses 9–18)

In the natural amphitheatre created by the colonnades and the ready audience provided by the 'disabled people' (verse 3) anyone who had been healed would have become the centre of attention. But in the case of this lame man it is not his healing that caused the stir but the fact that he now carried his mat on the Sabbath. The Jewish leaders reminded him, 'It is the Sabbath; the law forbids you to carry your mat.'

The *Mishnah* lists thirty-nine classes of work that are forbidden on the Sabbath (*Shabbath* 7:2) and hints that the list is incomplete because these are only 'the main classes of work'. These regulations can only be described as devious. For instance it wasn't wrong to borrow wine or oil on the Sabbath providing you didn't use the phrase 'lend them to me', as this would imply it was a transaction, and that would be work (*Shabbath* 23:1). You were forbidden to carry anything in your hands or on your shoulder on the Sabbath, but if you could contrive to balance it on the back of your hand or hold it in your mouth, that was allowed because it would only be work if you carried it in the normal way (*Shabbath* 10:3).

John 5:16–30

Healing and life come through the Son

Jesus gives a systematic statement about his unity with the Father, his divine work and his authority to judge.

We have already noticed that John's phrase 'the Jews' (verse 10) was a code he used to refer to the 'Jewish leaders who were opposed to Jesus'. This group is about to come into focus again, because the man who had been lame for thirty-eight years was healed 'on the Sabbath' and on account of this they began to persecute Jesus (verse 16).

Jesus the Sabbath, the Father and his work

In this section we have the most systematic statement to be found anywhere in this gospel on the relationship between Jesus and the Father, and his understanding of the work the Father had called him to do.

The Sabbath

Jesus doesn't refer directly to the Sabbath but to his Father: 'My Father is always at his work to this very day, and I, too, am working' (verse 17). After creation God rested (Genesis 2:2–3), but his resting had to do with creation, not everything else. He still had to sustain the universe. And the attitude of Jesus to the Sabbath springs from this. On a purely human level, you could say that the fate of Jesus was sealed at this point. In human terms this conversation cost him his life; the Jewish leaders never forgave him (verses 16–18).

Jesus equal with the Father

Jesus calls 'God his own Father, making himself equal with God' (verse 18). And he goes on to say, 'I tell you the truth, the Son can do nothing by himself'. Notice the 'I tell you the truth' phrase which precedes a double negative, making it a very emphatic statement. It strains the English, but it literally reads, 'The Son cannot do nothing'.

The Father loves the Son

The relationship between the Father and Jesus is one of love, 'For the Father loves the Son and shows him all he does' (verse 20). The next phrase about 'greater things' is hotly debated, but in context it is difficult to see that it means more than the 'things' Jesus is about to explain (verses 21–30), such as raising the dead and judgment.

Raising the dead

Jesus points out that the Father will raise the dead (verse 21). The Jewish leaders are not likely to disagree with that (Ezekiel 37:13). However, he goes on to say, 'even so the Son gives life to whom he is pleased'. He then immediately takes this statement another step: 'I tell you the truth, a time is coming and has now come when the dead will hear the voice of the Son of God and those who hear will live.' Then he adds, 'Do not be amazed at this, for a time is coming when all who are in their graves will hear his voice and come out' (verse 28).

Judgment

The final subject in this amazing section is concerned with judgment. Jesus touched on it first when he said, 'the Father judges no-one, but has entrusted all judgment to the Son' (verse 22). This is a direct claim to divinity because only God is the 'Judge of the whole earth' (Genesis 18:25). Jesus then expands this idea, 'And he has given him authority to judge because he is the Son of Man . . . I judge only as I hear, and my judgment is just, for I seek not to please myself but him who sent me' (verses 27–30). Escape from judgment comes from our attitude to Jesus and to those who believe in him. Indeed they have already 'crossed over from death to life' (verse 24).

Not only does Jesus make no attempt to placate those who were unhappy with his healing on the Sabbath, he also makes it difficult for them to say, in the future, that they hadn't understood the nature of his claims.

Questions

1. How does Jesus justify his action of healing on the Sabbath? In what ways might this relate to our modern use of Sunday?
2. How far should Christians persuade non-believers to respect Sunday as holy?
3. How do Jesus' claims to divinity emerge in this section?

John 5:31–47

Jesus names his witnesses

When his authority is called into question Jesus assembles a powerful list of witnesses: the Father, John the Baptist, his works, the Bible, and lastly Moses.

The witness of the Father (verses 31–32)

'If I testify about myself, my testimony is not valid' (verse 31). If the claims of Jesus were only supported by his own word they would be unreliable, because God's revelation did not begin and end in him: it reaches its height in him, but if what he says is true it will be supported by the rest of revelation. Jesus said, 'There is another who testifies in my favour.' He doesn't go on to say who the 'other' was. But the 'who testifies' is in the present tense, so it was going on all the time for those who could discern it. If only the Jewish leaders had been able to see, they would perceive that the Father was witnessing through every bit of the life of Jesus.

The testimony of John the Baptist (verse 32)

'You . . . sent to John'; it was the Jewish leaders' idea to send a delegation to John the Baptist, so in a real sense John was their witness. You might have expected Jesus to say that John the Baptist bore witness to him; in fact, he says, 'he testified to the truth'.

The evidence of his work (verse 36)

The third witness is the 'work' that Jesus has been doing. In fact, it is a 'testimony weightier than that of John'. God was in everything that Jesus did. We have noticed that John sometimes uses the word 'sign' to describe the miracles of Jesus because they are not simply demonstrations of power, they have a deeper spiritual meaning. On other occasions John uses the word 'work', which is a more general word. Every bit of the life of Jesus, in all its variety – the miraculous and the non-miraculous – shows God at work.

The evidence of the Bible (verse 39)

The majority of the leaders were Pharisees, and 'You diligently study the Scriptures', states Jesus. He is quite clear about the evidence of the Bible: these 'Scriptures . . . testify about me'. Look at Luke 24:25–27 for the same idea.

Moses confirms all that Jesus is and does (verses 45–46)

The chapter concludes with an unexpected line of reasoning. It won't be Jesus who in the end will accuse the leaders, it will be Moses. And if they had only studied Moses as thoroughly as they said they had, they would have found that he spoke of Christ. 'If you believed Moses, you would believe me, for he wrote about me.'

Questions

1. What evidence could you find for Jesus' authority? Make a list and compare it with the five witnesses described here. Which arguments carry most weight for Christians and for unbelievers?

2. Why is verse 45 unexpected? What does it mean?
3. Can we prove that Jesus is God's Son? If not, what will impress unbelievers most, our way of life, our membership of the church, our profession of faith or what? Try to be specific.

John 6:1–15

The loaves and the fish

Jesus uses the picnic of a young boy to feed a huge crowd of people, a sign of his power over the natural world.

The setting for the miracle (verse 1)

Jesus and his disciples had crossed to 'the far shore of the Sea of Galilee (that is, the Sea of Tiberias)'. This stretch of water had at least four different names in Bible times. At the beginning of the New Testament it was known as the 'Sea of Galilee', but just before Jesus began his ministry Herod (Antipas) built a new town on the west shore (*c.* AD 20). He called it 'Tiberius' after Caesar and that quickly became the local name for the sea too. So John adds that name for any reader from that part of the world.

The problem (verses 2–9)

The other gospel writers give a few extra details. John, however, concentrates on the miracle and the problem that gave rise to it which was the 'great crowd'. The crowd consisted of 'five thousand men' (verse 10) so, with women and children, a vast number of people needed to be fed. For a pessimist like Philip, the money from 'eight months' wages would not buy enough bread for each one to have a bite'. Andrew was more of an optimist, and although he knew 'five small barley loaves and two small fish' was not enough, at least it was a beginning. 'Barley loaves' were the cheapest form of bread, and the 'fish' were 'cooked, or prepared fish'. The Sea of Galilee teemed with these tiny creatures which were pickled and exported across the Roman Empire as a convenience food. So the young boy had *five pickled fishburgers* from *MacLevi's*, a typical 'packed lunch' of the area!

What happened (verses 10–11)

Jesus, having got the people to sit down, gave thanks and then they were given 'as much (food) as they wanted' (verse 11). You have to distort the details of the narrative to suggest that (1) the little boy's offering made everyone else open their picnic baskets, or that (2) what took place was a 'fellowship meal', a forerunner of the communion service. The only explanation that fits the facts is that this was a 'miraculous sign' (verse 14). And that is what John wants us to see.

The leftovers (verses 12–15)

'When they had all had enough to eat', the word is literally 'replete, and had their fill', Jesus told the disciples, 'Gather the pieces that are left over' and they 'filled twelve baskets'. The 'basket' was the wicker container that a traveller used for carrying food. It has given us our English word 'coffin'. They were about the size of a large shopping basket and were coffin-shaped; that is, their top and bottom were the same size, and they were at their widest two-thirds of the way up.

The miracle so impressed the people that they said, 'Surely this is the Prophet who is to come into the world'. And Jesus, 'knowing that they intended to come and make him king by force, withdrew' (verse 16). The Jews hated having their country occupied by the Romans and there is no doubt that they wanted the Messiah to come and liberate them. They expected Jesus to be a military redeemer, but he couldn't possibly be that. This is an age-old problem; people try to manipulate Jesus into doing what they want him to do, and the result is that they lose what he wants to be in their lives.

Questions

1. How have people sought to account for the miracle described here? What is 'the only explanation that fits the facts'? Are you convinced?
2. Are our churches responsible today to feed the hungry? How far should we expect miraculous help and how far are we responsible for the details?
3. What 'age-old problem' does this event lead to? Why does Jesus refuse the opportunity held out to him, to be acclaimed as king?

John 6:16–28

Looking for Jesus

Jesus appears to be playing cat and mouse with both the disciples and the crowd. He seems to be testing the seriousness of their search for the truth.

The storm at sea (verses 16–19)

At evening the disciples 'got into a boat and set off across the lake for Capernaum'. Two of the other gospel writers tell us that Jesus 'made his disciples' get into the boat (Matthew 14:22; Mark 6:45); literally, he 'compelled' them. This begs the question that if he knew that the people would try 'to make him king by force' (verse 15) why didn't he know about the storm? The answer is that he did, but calculated that the storm would be less damaging for the disciples than the razzmatazz of people wanting to make him king.

Miracle and reassurance (verses 20–21)

The preposition and the context clearly say that he walked 'on the water' (verse 19). Some point out that elsewhere the same words are translated 'by the sea' (21:1), but in both cases the context determines the meaning.

When 'they saw Jesus approaching the boat . . . they were terrified'. He immediately comforts them, 'It is I'. The disciples were reassured, because Jesus' words of comfort also confirmed his divine status. They were an emphatic pledge of the divine presence and reflect the 'I AM' of the Old Testament (Exodus 3:14). In today's everyday speech, it could be translated, 'It's me; I am'.

The crowd in search of satisfaction (verses 22–28)

As soon as Jesus was discovered on the other side of the sea, the crowd started to demand signs and a dialogue quickly developed which eventually became the sermon on the 'bread of life'.

It was a mixed crowd with at least five different focal points:

- There were the curious (verse 25);

- There were those who were seeking (verse 28);

- There were grumblers (verse 41);

- There were a few debaters (verse 52);

- There were those who decided that they could no longer follow Jesus (verse 66), the saddest group of all.

Sealed with God's seal (verse 27)

When the crowd discovered Jesus at Capernaum and began to question him, he replied, 'Do not work for food that spoils, but for food that endures to eternal life'. And Jesus goes on to say that this food can be given them by the 'Son of Man', the one to whom God has given his 'seal of approval'.

Apart from legal documents, seals are not used much in today's world. But in the days before people could read or write, a man's seal was his distinguishing mark; it was his authenticating stamp, ratifying who he was, and what belonged to him. 'Eternal life' can be found from the one who has been validated as the 'Son of Man' with God's 'seal'. We might add that Jesus has signed us as his guarantee. So we have his seal of approval.

Questions

1. Why were the disciples so terrified when they saw Jesus? What is remarkable about what he says to them in verse 20?
2. What does Jesus mean by 'food that endures to eternal life'? How can we get hold of such food for ourselves?
3. If God is in control of the elements of nature, why does he permit drought, floods, earthquakes and volcanic eruptions?

The 'I AM' sayings in John's gospel

The language of the New Testament is a 'reflexive' language. In such a language you don't need a pronoun; the verb tells you all you need to know. But occasionally John records Jesus using both the verb 'to be' and the pronoun 'I'; we have already had an example in this chapter.

Literally, Jesus said to the disciples as he approached the boat, 'I, I am; don't be afraid' (verse 20). There are seven occasions in this gospel where Jesus underlines his divinity by using both the verb and the pronoun together. They are called 'The I AM sayings'. The seven sayings are:

- 'I AM the bread of life' (6:35);

- 'I AM the light of the world' (8:12);

- 'I AM the gate for the sheep' (in older translations this is 'I AM the door') (10:7);

- 'I AM the good shepherd' (10:11);

- 'I AM the resurrection and the life' (11:25);

- 'I AM the way and the truth and the life' (14:6);

- 'I AM the vine' (15:1).

We have the first of these sayings in the next section: 'I am the bread of life'.

John 6:29–71

Jesus the bread of life

Jesus makes a dramatic claim which both disciples and crowd find very difficult to understand. This results in division between those who follow and those who desert Jesus.

Manna from heaven

The response of the crowd was that they wanted something much more tangible than someone who had been sealed by God. 'What miraculous sign will you give . . .? Our forefathers ate the manna in the desert' (verses 30–31). But Jesus insisted that it was not Moses who gave 'bread from heaven', but his 'Father' and he was still able to give 'true bread from heaven' to those who wanted it. When Jesus specifically points to this bread they don't understand him (verse 33), even though they wanted what he had to offer. Now his claim to divinity is clear and emphatic, 'I am the bread of life.' Literally, 'I, I am the bread of life.' The idea is repeated through the chapter sometimes with a slight variation: 'I am the bread that came down from heaven' (verse 41); 'I am the bread of life' (verse 48); 'I am the living bread' (verse 51).

How to enjoy this bread

Surprisingly, when Jesus first stated that he was 'the bread of life', he didn't say 'eat', but 'come'. Human metaphors can never be exact about a spiritual experience. We 'come' (verse 35), or we 'eat' (verse 51), or we 'believe' (verse 29); they all imply the same thing. Indeed, in this chapter the word 'believe' is used more than the other two which is probably why Augustine, the fourth-century bishop, said, 'If you believe in Christ you have eaten him'. The important thing however is that we have experienced him, and can see that he is able to satisfy us totally. We 'will never go hungry' and we 'will never be thirsty' (verse 35). Jesus couldn't stress more strongly his ability to meet the needs of disciples who really 'get their teeth' into him.

Part of the satisfaction will come from the sense of

▶ security at being chosen by God: 'all that the Father gives me will come to me' (verses 37, 44, 65); and

▶ being identified with him and he with us: 'Whoever eats my flesh and drinks my blood remains in me, and I in him' (verse 56).

Some stop following Jesus

There are three different 'stumbling-blocks' mentioned in this chapter. Any one of these, or a combination of all three, could cause disciples to fall away.

▶ The essentially spiritual nature of Jesus' message led him to say of some, 'You are looking for me . . . because you ate the loaves and had your fill' (verse 26). Jesus knew that all these particular followers wanted was a full stomach.

▶ Others couldn't accept the claim of Jesus to be divine, 'Is this not Jesus, the son of Joseph, whose father and mother we know? How can he now say, "I came down from heaven"?' (verse 42).

▶ But clearly the 'hard teaching' (verse 60) that threw so many was the need to be totally involved with Jesus; whoever 'eats (his) flesh and drinks (his) blood' – again 'to get their teeth' into him.

Once when John Wesley was talking to someone who thought he could be a Christian all by himself, Wesley picked up a pair of tongs and took a hot coal out of the fire. Almost immediately it started to go out. Wesley didn't even have to draw the analogy. It is difficult, if not impossible, to get a single coal to continue burning by itself. Most people fall away from the church today because they fail to meet with God's people and therefore lose the warmth of Christian fellowship. Or, more seriously still, they fail to meet with Jesus regularly. We will see later that Jesus says that he 'is the vine and we are the branches' (p. 160). We need to sustain that relationship to make sure 'the sap' keeps flowing.

Peter confesses that Jesus is Lord

Because of the 'disciples (who) turned back' Jesus asked the twelve, 'You do not want to leave too, do you?' Another feature of the New Testament language is that you can ask a question in one way to receive a negative reply and ask in a different way if you expect a positive reply. The question to the twelve looked for the answer, 'No'; Jesus is confident of his close band of followers. Indeed Peter chimes up with, 'Lord, to whom shall we go? You have the words of eternal life. We believe and know that you are the Holy One of God' (verses 68–69).

Judas Iscariot

Jesus recognized that while what Peter said was true for eleven, it wasn't true for all twelve. 'One' of them was 'a devil!' He was speaking about Judas, the son of Simon Iscariot. 'Iscariot' is a place-name meaning 'Man of Kerioth'; there are two 'Kerioths' in the Bible, one in Judah (Joshua 15:25) and the other in Moab (Jeremiah 48:24). This makes 'Judas' the only one of the twelve who didn't come from Galilee.

Questions

1. What is the reality behind the idea of eating 'the bread of life'? To what extent have you experienced this?
2. What does the author identify as 'three different stumbling-blocks in this chapter that could cause disciples to fall away'? How may these be avoided?
3. What is it about Jesus that leads Peter and the rest of the Twelve to stay with him after the others have left? How far are you able to identify with what Peter says?
4. What do you make of the fact that Jesus deliberately chose Judas Iscariot, whom he describes as 'a devil', to be one of his closest followers?

John 7:1–24

Who is this Jesus?

**Again Jesus has both disciples and the crowd
guessing about where he is and who he is.
Curiosity and controversy increase.**

The feast of the tabernacles

On four occasions in this chapter John points to
'the Feast of Tabernacles' (verses 2, 8, 14, 37).
Notice he doesn't call it 'a feast' but '*the* Jewish Feast'. A casual
reading of the New Testament could make you think that Passover
was the most important feast in the annual round of festivals, but
this was not so. All adult males had to attend the three major
festivals each year (Exodus 23:17) and Passover was simply one of
these. The others were the 'Feast of the Harvest', which celebrated
the gathering in of the first fruits, and the 'Feast of Ingathering, or
Tabernacles', which marked the completion of the harvest.

The Jews were an agricultural people and Passover was
important because it spoke of the nation's redemption and
beginning. 'Tabernacles' marked the high point of the year
because with the harvest safely in, they could look forward to
another year.

The name 'Tabernacles' referred to the custom of building little
leafy tents which the people erected in their courtyards or on
their flat roofs. These temporary dwellings reminded them of
God's goodness as they had travelled through the Wilderness to
the Promised Land. We are not certain how long the festival
lasted. It seemed to have been seven days (Leviticus 23:34;
Deuteronomy 16:13, 15), but it is possible that at some time it
was extended to include an eighth day.

Jesus and his human family

The time would come when Jesus' brothers would be counted among his disciples (Acts 1:14), but during most of his earthly life they regarded him with scepticism and suspicion. Here, as the feast approached they urged him to go to Judea (verse 3). The reason for this seemed to be sarcastic disbelief. 'You ought to leave here and go to Judea, so that your disciples may see the miracles you do'. The disciples had been present at all the miracles so far; so clearly 'Show yourself to the world' sprang from his brothers' disbelief.

Jesus responded by telling his brothers, 'The right time for me has not yet come'. We've already noticed that throughout this gospel Jesus talks about his time 'having not yet come'. These statements will be made right up to the night before his crucifixion when he will say that it 'had come' (12:23; 13:1).

The Jerusalem mob

Some time after 'his brothers had left for the feast' Jesus 'went also, not publicly, but in secret' (verse 10). This sounds rather mysterious, but that wasn't the intention. We are simply being told that Jesus didn't travel in one of the large official caravans of pilgrims heading for Jerusalem. He chose to be inconspicuous, because people were already saying 'Where is that man?' Among the Jerusalem mob there was a wide difference of opinion about him; some said, 'He is a good man', and others that 'he deceives the people' (verse 12).

The pilgrims in the temple

Once Jesus arrived in Jerusalem, he didn't attempt to hide, but went openly to the temple courts and began to teach. His ability as a teacher caused astonishment (see below *The education of Jesus*).

Questions

1. What significance do you think there is in the fact that the events of this chapter take place at the Feast of Tabernacles?
2. Why is it so difficult to speak of our deepest beliefs to members of our own family? Share, in your group, encouragements and disappointments.
3. What lay behind the enthusiasm of Jesus' brothers for him to go to the Feast? Why does Jesus say 'no' to them and then seem to change his mind?
4. Jesus appears to the world as a mysterious and enigmatic figure. How can we make use of this intriguing aspect of his reputation in our witness and evangelism?

The education of Jesus

We need to look at the whole question of education in Bible times. Notice:

▶ It was only available for boys. And as with all oral traditions, vast amounts of material would have to be learnt by heart. A young Jewish boy would learn a large part of the Law (the first five books of the Old Testament). He would certainly be expected to recite large parts of it when he became of age on his twelfth birthday. The only further education available would be to go to a rabbinical school and personally sit at the feet of a rabbi. This is what was meant by 'having studied' (verse 15).

▶ The surprising ability of Jesus was not his knowledge, but the thoroughness, depth and ease with which he applied it.

▶ His teaching must have been impressive because 'the Jews'

(verse 15), the group who were hostile to him, were 'amazed' by it. They said, 'How did this man get such learning without having studied?'

▶ Jesus responded by saying that his teaching wasn't his own, and if anyone had been sincere about doing God's will they would have discovered that his teaching came 'from God' (verse 17).

▶ When Jesus turned to speak about 'Moses' (verse 19) he was not changing the subject; at the heart of all Jewish teaching was the Law. Most rabbinical teaching would be an interpretation and application of the Law.

▶ The 'sabbath' (verse 23) was now the central issue between the leaders and Jesus. The passage points to the fact that the leaders had not recognized this and so they had not followed the argument.

John 7:25–36

Confusion deepens

The people, the Pharisees, the police and the politicians (verses 45–52) all join in the debate without any light appearing.

The Jerusalemites

We meet another group described as 'some of the people of Jerusalem' (verse 25). They were also amazed at Jesus' teaching and said, 'Isn't this the man they are trying to kill?' They presumed he was speaking publicly because the authorities had concluded that he was the Christ. Jesus 'cried out' (verse 28); he wanted everyone to hear what he said. Again he repeats a central theme of this gospel, 'Yes, you know me, and you know where I am from. I am not here on my own, but he who sent me is true'. It is not surprising that they tried to 'seize him' (verse 30).

The temple police

Policemen of every age are among the most realistic members of the human race. They've heard every excuse, seen every sort of accident and witnessed the result of every known crime. So carefully note the reaction of these policemen, 'No-one ever spoke the way this man does' (verse 46).

Questions

1. In what ways do the different groups of people described by John react to the teaching of Jesus? Can you point to parallels today?
2. How far should Christians obey, believe, respect and support the authorities, both political and churchl? How can we decide who is right?

Background to the Feast

We have noticed that everybody built little leafy tents at the time of 'Tabernacles'. The first night of the festival was called The Feast of the Illumination and involved the erecting of four enormous candelabra in the Court of the Women. We will look more thoroughly at these in the next chapter.

The main ceremony in the temple each day was an enacted prayer for rain. When the people gathered in the temple each day they would be holding an *etrog* (a citrus fruit) in their left hand which represented 'the land of good things' into which the Lord had brought them. In their right hand, they had a *lulab*, a little bundle of leafy branches of willow and myrtle together with a palm frond. These represented the leafy bivouacs they had used on the journey to the promised land.

The priest would be holding a small golden jug. The people would accompany him down through the streets of Jerusalem and out through the Water Gate where he would fill the jug in the Pool of Siloam. As the priest straightened up the people would recite: 'With joy (we) will draw water from the wells of salvation' (Isaiah 12:3). The procession would then return to the temple, led by the priest while the people sang the *Hallel* (Praise) psalms (Psalms 113–118), shaking their *lulabs* and accompanied by dancers and musicians playing flutes.

Once back in the temple, the priest would pour the water into a bowl set beside the altar. Because it was said to be a blessing if you could actually see the water poured out, the priest would pause while holding the jug as high as he could. Everybody was aware that unless God gave rain in the coming months there would be no celebration next year.

John 7:37–52

Drink the Spirit!

Jesus goes public with his teaching on the Holy Spirit. Nicodemus, who has heard Jesus on the subject in private (chapter 3), intervenes to save Jesus from arrest.

The words 'a loud voice' (verse 37) spoke of a shout that was intended to make the maximum number of people hear what was said. Jesus draws the attention of the crowd  from the central event of Tabernacles to himself: 'If anyone is thirsty, let him come to me and drink.' He points to himself as the source of Holy Spirit blessing. It is not clear whether there are three or four verbs in verse 37; it depends where you put the punctuation.

The secret of Holy Spirit blessing

We are looking at the days before Pentecost. Since Pentecost the Holy Spirit has been given to every believer. But there can be no harm in working through the steps to blessing that Jesus suggests to the people here. They are

- *to thirst*. The word describes a deep inner longing (even craving) for something that only Jesus can give. Then they are

- *to come*. The general movement of their lives must now be in God's direction. This is followed by

- *to drink*. They are to appropriate all that God has for them. And finally

➤ *to believe.* They have to take their stand (believe) all that God has said.

A difficulty

There are several problems in verse 38. Not least, exactly from whom would the 'streams of living water . . . flow from within'? Would it be believers or Jesus? Because most people think it was from Jesus, they put 'he who believes' with the other verbs. But there is a sense that when the believer is truly living close to Christ, the blessing flows from that relationship to others. And the grammar demands that the 'him' from whom the 'streams of living waters . . . flow' is the same as the one who 'thirsts' and 'believes'. So it can't possibly be Jesus.

But the difficulties increase when you try to find a verse that speaks of living water flow from within either Christ or the believer. It is at this point that John adds a note about the Holy Spirit (verse 39).

A big difficulty

It is only when you come to verse 39 that you encounter the big problem of the chapter. It is smoothed over by the translators. Literally John says: 'For it was not yet spirit . . .' But the translators try to make sense out of this by saying, 'Up to that time the (Holy) Spirit had not been given . . .' – yet that was not true. The Holy Spirit had been given in the Old Testament to specific people at particular times. And in the New Testament we know that John the Baptist, Elizabeth and Simeon had been given the Holy Spirit in extraordinary measure (Luke 1:15, 41; 2:25).

The era of the Spirit

The clue to a right understanding of verse 39 is the word 'glorified'. John nearly always used it in connection with the death of Jesus. 'The hour has come for the Son of Man to be glorified' (12:23; see also 13:31). So what John is saying is: 'By

99

this he meant the Spirit, whom those who believed in him were yet to receive. For it was not yet (the era of) the Holy Spirit, because Jesus hadn't died and therefore Pentecost which would inaugurate the epoch of the Spirit hadn't taken place.'

So it was on the last, the great day of Tabernacles, as the priest reached as high as he could with his little jug, that Jesus cried out, drawing the attention of the crowd to himself. In effect he said that he was the source of Holy Spirit blessing: 'If anyone is thirsty, let him come to me and drink' (verse 37). John adds the note confirming that Jesus was talking about the Spirit; who would be available to the whole church after Pentecost.

How can we 'drink the Spirit'?

In the Old Testament God spoke through Jeremiah and said, 'My people . . . have forsaken me, *the spring of living water*, and have dug . . . cisterns, broken cisterns that cannot hold water' (Jeremiah 2:13). Modern men and women rush to fill the emptiness of their lives with a whole galaxy of stimulants and depressants, only to find that they don't satisfy. These things are 'broken cisterns that cannot hold water'. But when we develop a relationship with Jesus Christ, we are coming to *'the spring of living water'*. He truly satisfies, and 'eternal life' will 'well up' within us (John 4:14; p. 66).

The politicians (verses 45–52)

We have met Nicodemus already and we now see him as an MP on his own ground. The other leaders were astonished at what the temple guards had said and could only conclude, 'You mean he has deceived you also?' (verse 47). Nicodemus pointed out that the Law required that people should be heard before they were condemned. But the other politicians were in no mood for legal niceties and ask if Nicodemus was a Galilean too, pointing out that no prophet had ever come from Galilee. That was not strictly true, but more to the point was the fact that God could raise up prophets from wherever he chose.

The major part of this chapter is a series of verdicts about Jesus. And you could say that John has his tongue in his cheek as he shows these to us. When the hostile leaders say, 'How did this man get such learning?' (verse 15), you need to remember that we have been told that Jesus is 'the Word' (the Reason of God) who has existed since long before the beginning of space–time–history (1:1–3).

Questions

1. What can we learn from the 'steps to blessing' which Jesus talks about in verse 37?
2. What is the 'big problem' in this chapter? How may this difficulty be resolved? How does it affect us today?
3. Is God's Holy Spirit at work equally everywhere? What might limit his activities?

John 8:1–11

Caught in the act!

Jesus is caught in a trap, challenged to choose between law and love. His response demonstrates that God requires both purity and mercy.

Jesus' teaching programme was rudely interrupted and a dishevelled woman thrust before him. When the woman caught in adultery was brought before Jesus, several questions leap to mind, not least, 'Where was the man involved in this?' But such was the chauvinism of the Jews of this period, that he was very unlikely to appear. His crime would somehow be reduced to the lesser charge of *fornication*, which didn't carry the death penalty. There were three capital offences; *idolatry*, *adultery* and *murder*. In each case the penalty would be death by stoning (Deuteronomy 22:21).

The group of men who had brought the woman were not really interested in her sexual adventure; their aim was to 'trap' Jesus 'in order to have a basis for accusing him' (verse 6). If their concern had been one of morality, having caught the couple, they would not have questioned Jesus about stoning both of them, because that was what the law required (Leviticus 20:10; Deuteronomy 22:22).

As always in such debates, Jesus was able to take care of himself. His answer puts the onus back on the accusers. It is intriguing to note that if Jesus had said, 'Stone her', he would immediately have fallen foul of the Roman authorities. And if he had said, 'Don't stone her', then the Jews would have caused trouble. Of course, in one sense he did say, 'Stone her,' so no-one would ever be able to say he didn't uphold the law. However, by choosing his words carefully, he was determining that no execution would take place that day.

Jesus called her 'woman' (verse 10); we have already noticed that this wasn't as cold as it sounds to us (p. 48). She also referred to him as, 'Sir', literally, 'Lord', so it could be argued that she had the beginnings of faith (1 Corinthians 12:3).

You may feel that Jesus is being soft on adultery here, but the thrust of the passage is that it is an example of God's forgiveness. The other side of the coin is that Jesus is not going to let the men get away with pointing a finger at the woman without pointing it at themselves. In the other gospels Jesus deals with the loose attitude of thinking and says that he even regards lustful *thoughts* as adultery as well as actual fornication (Matthew 5:28). So it is not difficult to imagine what he thought about the man not being charged with adultery here.

If the media are to be believed, adultery is no longer regarded as sinful or even wrong if both partners 'feel' right. But Jesus teaching is for all time. Two facts stand out. Adultery is always wrong. Penitent adulterers can always be forgiven.

As to what Jesus wrote 'on the ground with his finger' (verse 6), we are left completely in the dark. The finger of God has written in recorded history. In the story of Daniel God's finger appeared at Belshazzar's Feast and wrote four Persian words on the wall, 'MENE, MENE, TEKEL, PARSIN . . . you have been weighed on the scales and found wanting' (Daniel 5:25, 27). If that wasn't what Jesus wrote on the ground, it was certainly what the men felt he was saying, because they 'began to go away one at a time' (verse 9).

Questions

---

1. In what way is this accusation a 'trap' for Jesus?
2. Why might this incident *not* reoccur in your church today? Have our moral standards become too lax or is our toleration a virtue?
3. How does Jesus deal with the fact of the woman's wrong-doing? What can we learn for our own situation? Share examples.

The problem of the text

Most translations have a footnote or a heading which says that 'the earliest and most reliable manuscripts do not have John 7:53 – 8:11'. These verses are only found in one major document. When they are included in less important texts they are always put in a different place in the narrative. Scholars also point out that the phrase 'the teachers of the law' (verse 3) is not one that John would normally use. It sounds much more like one of the earlier gospel writers. However, the account does have a ring of authenticity, and it may well be that the early church simply thought that the story encouraged adultery, so they left it out. But the theme of the story is *forgiveness*, which is a very different matter.

John 8:12

The source of all light

———

In the reflected light of the great candelabrum in Jerusalem Jesus claims to be 'the light of the world'.

The stage is set

After 'the last and greatest day of the Feast' (7:37), when some wanted to arrest Jesus (7:44), he 'went to the Mount of Olives. At dawn he appeared again in the temple courts . . . near the place where the offerings were put' (8:1, 2, 20). This was where Jesus loved to teach because it always guaranteed a crowd. When 'he sat down' (verse 2) it was a sign that a sermon was about to begin. Then came the interruption discussed in the last study.

Now as 'Jesus spoke again to the people' he would have to do little more than point over his shoulder at one of the huge candelabra and say, 'I am the light of the world'.

The light of the world

It was an astonishing claim, made even more so against the background of Tabernacles. The candelabra provided such a powerful light that it was said you couldn't find a dark corner anywhere in Jerusalem during the Feast of the Illumination. And even if you could, you wouldn't be able to sleep because of the noise of the musicians and dancers.

The candelabra represented the glory of God which was seen by the Israelites as they travelled towards the promised land; it appeared as 'a pillar of cloud' by day and 'a pillar of fire' by night (Exodus 13:21).

Jesus was saying, why put up these candelabra to represent God's glory, when 'I am the light of the world'? Jesus used the emphasis we have already noticed by adding a second pronoun to the verb. He said, 'I–I am', underlining his claim to divinity by echoing God's words, and using one of God's names (Exodus 3:14).

A promise with a condition

If the crowd were astonished by the claim, they must have been equally challenged by the promise, 'Whoever follows me will never walk in darkness, but will have the light of life.'

'Follow me'

Instead of the darkness of error, deception and death, 'the light of life' could now mark the lives of the followers of Jesus. The early disciples literally 'followed' him from place to place (Luke 8:1–3), but the word was quickly used to describe those who *adhered* to his teaching. So, any disciples who followed him would 'never walk in darkness, but will have the light of life' with them wherever they go.

There is a slight variation of meaning in the verb 'to follow', but there are similarities too. We can 'follow'

▶ as a soldier follows a King,
▶ as a slave follows a master,

- as a citizen follows the laws of the land,

- as a scholar follows a teacher or

- as a young man follows the wisdom of an older man.

At the heart of all these is the idea of *commitment*. Followers of Jesus today must be as committed as the early disciples. We don't have to move from place to place, but we need to stick to his teaching; and be his followers wherever we are.

Questions

1. What is so astonishing about Jesus' claim to be 'the light of the world'?
2. What does it mean in practice for someone to *follow* Jesus?
3. Which aspects of Jesus' teaching do you find it hard to stick to? Why?

More background to the Feast of Tabernacles

We saw in the last chapter that all this took place at 'Tabernacles' (7:2, 10, 14, 37). And we noted that the first night of Tabernacles was the Feast of the Illumination and involved four enormous candelabra being erected in the Court of the Women. Their size can be gauged from the fact that their fuel reservoir contained 'four and a half gallons of oil' to provide light for one night. The wicks were made from the discarded robes of the priests which were plaited together and said to be 'the thickness of a man's thigh'. We are told that on that first night of Tabernacles, 'there was not a courtyard in Jerusalem that did not reflect the light'. And 'men of piety and good works used to dance before them with burning torches in their hands, singing songs and praises, and countless Levites played harps, lyres, cymbals and trumpets and instruments of music (*Mishna Sukkah* 5:2–3).

As on all sacred occasions, work was prohibited. So although the lamps wouldn't be used again that year, they would remain in place in the Court of the Women, until the day after the festival. Then they would be taken down, dismantled and put away for another year.

The place where the offerings were put

The treasury consisted of thirteen chests known as 'the trumpets' because of their shape. They had a small round opening at the top for the money and swept out to a large circular base on which they stood. The first and second trumpets were used by adult male Jews for their annual temple tax. The third and fourth by women who had recently given birth; they would put in the price of two pigeons to be made ceremonially clean. The fifth was for anyone who wanted to give an offering towards the wood for the temple fires. The sixth was for offerings that helped provide incense and the seventh to maintain the temple's gold plate. If God had been good to you and you simply wanted to give a thank offering, the *remaining six* trumpets were there for that purpose.

John 8:13–59

A fierce debate

As Jesus is urged by the Pharisees to divulge his true nature their response becomes increasingly violent.

A valid testimony (verses 13–20)

The opponents of Jesus hadn't really listened to what he was saying. Instead they turned to the rules governing evidence and said, 'Your testimony is not valid'. Their reason for saying this was that Jesus was appearing as his own witness, which was not allowed. But Jesus insists that even according to their law, his testimony was legal, because his Father was the 'other witness' (verse 18).

Going away (verses 21–24)

John had a special interest in the 'eternal life' that Jesus offered to his followers. Without Jesus the people would 'die in (their) sin'. Jesus told the Pharisees this would happen to them because they had lost their opportunity. He was 'going away'; he was 'from above' and they were 'from below'.

The Son of Man lifted up (verse 28)

When the Pharisees asked him, 'Who are you?' he replied that he was 'just what I have been claiming all along' (verse 25). But they didn't seem to understand, so he continued, 'When you have lifted up the Son of Man, then you will know I am the one I claim to be'. We have already noticed that John used the verb 'to lift up' in an unusual way (p. 58). John uses it four times and on each occasion it refers to the crucifixion. Presumably it does so here as well, so the men who would lift Jesus up by nailing him to the cross would one day appreciate the heavenly exultation and glory that belonged to him. And they would know that 'the one who sent (him)' had 'not left (him) alone' (verse 29).

The disciples' freedom (verses 31–36)

To the group who 'had believed him' Jesus said, 'If you hold to my teaching, you are really my disciples. Then you will know the truth, and the truth will set you free'.

The point Jesus is making is that commitment doesn't bring an enclosed treadmill experience, but liberty. The group insists that they were already free because they were 'Abraham's descendants' (verse 33). Jesus replied, 'everyone who sins is a slave to sin.' If Jesus had set them free they were 'free indeed', because he alone could free them from the slavery to sin.

The devil and his children (verses 38–50)

Jesus agrees that physically they were descendants of Abraham, but their conduct was quite another matter. Abraham's real offspring 'would do the things Abraham did' whereas they were 'ready to kill' him, so they must 'belong to (their) father, the devil'.

Before Abraham was (verses 51–59)

Many people who can't win an argument resort to unkind words and that is what happens here. 'Aren't we right in saying that you are a Samaritan and demon-possessed?' (verse 48). In response Jesus says, 'I tell you the truth, if anyone keeps my word, he will never see death'. By 'word' Jesus meant the whole body of his teaching (see also verses 31, 37, 43). Jesus insists that any disciple who accepted his teaching and acted upon it would 'never see death'. Again his opponents are upset and protest that 'Abraham died and so did the prophets'. Now in the most unequivocal way Jesus asserts his divinity: 'before Abraham was born, I am', and the crowds responded by picking up 'stones to stone him'. To claim to be equal with God was blasphemy, punishable by death.

Questions

1. How does Jesus answer the objection that he is appearing as his own witness? Do you think his opponents were convinced?
2. What does it mean to be 'free indeed'? How far is it true of your own life? Share experiences in the group.
3. Why were Jesus' opponents unable to accept what he was telling them? Apply your answer to your own efforts at witness and evangelism.

John 9:1–23

Light for a blind man

The Jews do not believe that it was possible for a man born blind to be healed. When it happens they have to resort to desperate measures.

This is the only miracle in the gospels where the person involved has suffered since birth. There are two such miracles in the Acts of the Apostles: the healing of the lame man at the 'Beautiful gate' (Acts 3:2) and the healing of the impotent man at Lystra (Acts 14:8).

We need to notice the geographical setting for the chapter. We were told at the end of the last chapter about Jesus 'slipping away from the temple grounds' (8:59). So he encountered this man somewhere in Jerusalem and told him to 'wash in the Pool of Siloam' (verse 7; see p. 113).

A blind man is healed (verses 1–7)

The disciples were struggling with one of life's great mysteries; the problem of suffering. The rabbis said, 'There is no death without sin and no suffering without iniquity.' So the disciples asked, 'Rabbi [Jesus], who sinned, this man or his parents?' But we need to be very careful to avoid the trap of thinking this way. It is wrong to blame God or the person involved (or their parents for that matter) for any of life's unpleasant experiences. Suffering comes as a direct result of living in what Gerard Manley Hopkins called 'a bent world', a world which has been contaminated and warped by sin.

The ability of Jesus to heal this man pointed to the fact that he was the Messiah. Later the man said, 'Nobody has ever heard of opening the eyes of a man born blind' (verse 32). This was true, but the Old Testament speaks of the Messiah having this ability (Isaiah 29:18; 35:5; 42:6–7; Psalm 146:8).

Reaction to the healing (verses 8–43)

The neighbours were curious (verse 8)

Whenever and wherever Jesus works there is curiosity; it might be a healing, or it could be our own conversion, or the conversion of a friend. People are bound to be interested. This is one reason why personal testimony is so powerful.

The Pharisees are contemptuous (verses 16–18)

The man was taken to the Pharisees who made no attempt to hide their contempt at the idea that God would heal an outcast of society and use someone like Jesus, whom they considered a 'sinner'. Note the danger of a doctrinaire attitude to truth. We must come to the Bible with an open mind and not try to squeeze its teaching into any theories we already hold.

The Pharisees finally asked the man what he thought about Jesus. He replied that Jesus was a 'prophet'. But the Pharisees won't acknowledge that Jesus had restored the man's sight and send for his parents.

The parents are reluctant to point to Jesus as the healer (verse 20)

To understand the situation we need to imagine ourselves in a tiny community dominated by religious leaders who are unwilling to accept that God was working through Jesus Christ. If the parents were to become unacceptable to the leaders they would be turned 'out of the synagogue'. Then nobody would accept them; the shops wouldn't accept their custom and their neighbours wouldn't speak to them. They would be like lepers, outcasts of society. Fear therefore made them prevaricate; they could not deny that the man was their son, but that was all. 'We know he is our son,' the parents answered, 'and we know he was born blind. But how he can see now, or who opened his eyes, we don't know. Ask him. He is of age; he will speak for himself'.

Apart from the understandable fear of the man's parents, they present us with a good example to follow when speaking about spiritual things. A simple bold statement (i.e. 'I believe in Jesus Christ') is much more powerful than a whole string of theological arguments.

Questions

1. What trap are the disciples in danger of falling into at the beginning of chapter 9? To what extent are you inclined to go down the same path?
2. What can we learn from the various reactions to the healing of

the blind man? Consider the reactions of the disciples, the Pharisees, the parents, and the man himself.

3. Consider various forms of 'alternative healing' (e.g. chiropractic, herbal cures, acupuncture, laying on of hands in Christ's name . . .). How does each compare to 'scientific' medicine?

The Pool of Siloam

This pool was like the Eiffel Tower in Paris; it was an amazing piece of engineering that had become a landmark of the city. Jerusalem was almost impregnable. So far as food was concerned, it could sustain a seige almost indefinitely. The problem was water because there was no source in the city. The nearest supply was the Spring of Gihon across the Kidron Valley to the east.

Just before Sennacherib attacked Jerusalem in 701 BC, King Hezekiah decided to build a tunnel to bring water from the spring right into the city. He set thirty-three men to work cutting through solid rock. To facilitate the process, they were divided into two groups, digging the tunnel from both ends. It is not surprising that without modern cutting equipment they followed the softer fissures of rock and zig-zagged towards each other. Hence a tunnel that should have been no more than 340 metres in length was in fact 540 metres. Strictly speaking the tunnel was called 'Siloam' or 'sent' (verse 7), but from the earliest times the pool was known as 'Siloam' too (Isaiah 8:6; for details of the building of the tunnel see 2 Chronicles 32:2–8; Isaiah 2:9–11; 2 Kings 20:20).

'Rabbi' (verse 2)

'Rabbi' means 'My Great One'. There is no modern equivalent, although the original meaning of the French 'Monsieur' is similar. In theory 'Rabbi' could be used of anyone in a variety of occupations, but in practice it was only used for teachers. And that is what it means hre.

John 9:24–41

Spiritual darkness for the 'enlightened'

As the plot thickens it becomes clear that the ones who claim to be spiritually enlightened are wilfully refusing to see the truth before their eyes.

The formerly blind man was too ecstatic to deny anything. He hadn't seen who the healer was, but he couldn't deny that he had been healed. He was indignant that he had to explain it all over again.

The Pharisees lose their tempers

The Pharisees 'hurled insults at him' (verse 28). Literally, they 'scolded him in a loud and abrasive manner'. If we are in any form of leadership we especially need to notice what is happening here. In any structure, the leaders will find some people disagree with them. There is nothing basically wrong with this.

Unless we are dealing with a major doctrine, people are entitled to their opinion; that is one of the foundational principles of the Reformation. The healed man was right to be indignant about the way he had been treated. But the Pharisees were wrong to lose their tempers. The sad result was that they 'threw (the man) out' of the temple (verse 34). What the parents dreaded now happened to their son.

Jesus meets the healed man

John Chrysostom, the gifted preacher and writer of the fourth century, said, 'The Jews threw the man out of the temple, and the Lord of the temple found him.' It can't be expressed more clearly than that. The man moved from the wonder of being given sight to the place of worship. He said, ' "Lord I believe," and he worshipped him' (verse 38). The word 'worship' is the main New Testament word describing a 'moving forward to adore'.

Progress in titles

Notice the different titles that the man used to describe Jesus:

▶ 'The man they call Jesus' (verse 11).

▶ 'He is a prophet' (verse 17).

▶ 'Do you want to become his disciples, too?' (verse 27); implying that Jesus was already his master.

▶ ' "Lord, I believe," and he worshipped him' (verse 38). Again by implication he is saying, 'My Lord and my God.'

Questions

---

1. What do those in leadership need to notice about what happens here? Why?
2. Tease out the various meanings implied by the word 'blind' in verses 39–41. In what ways ought we to be 'blind'? In what ways should we hope to 'see'?
3. John's account demonstrates a clear progression in the man's understanding of who Jesus is. Can you trace a similar sequence in your own experience? Share with your group.

Son of Man

'Son of Man' was the title Jesus chose for himself. It comes eighty-two times in the New Testament and only once outside the gospels. That single exception was when Stephen was martyred. Stephen described how he saw the 'heaven open and the Son of Man standing at the right hand of God' (Acts 7:56). With that one exception, all other uses of 'Son of Man' come from the lips of Jesus, describing himself. Jesus spoke Aramaic, the local Hebrew dialect. In Aramaic 'Son of Man' isn't really a title, it is a way of saying 'a man'. If a rabbi was telling a story he might begin, 'There was a son of man' meaning 'There was a man'.

So when Jesus called himself 'Son of Man' he was thinking of himself as the representative man. There was nothing distinctive about Jesus in a national sense. He wasn't the 'son of a Jew' or the 'son of a carpenter', he was the 'son of man'. In the same way, although he fitted into his time and culture, it is difficult to say he was a man of the first century; he was a man of every century and of every age. He was the representative man; the 'son of man'.

John 10:1–18

The Good Shepherd

Jesus' celebrated teaching is not as simple as it looks. He is the shepherd but also the 'gate'. In both cases he is opposed to the false shepherds who are misleading the flock.

The parable (verses 1–6)

In Bible times sheep and shepherds were an everyday sight, so the teaching here would have been obvious. But this is not true today because most of us live in cities and, apart from the domestic sort, we can spend most of our lives without seeing a real animal.

Background

In the Old Testament there are several devastating passages about 'the shepherds of Israel who only take care of themselves' (Ezekiel 34:2); and 'Israel's watchmen (who) are blind' and who each cry, 'let me get wine! Let us drink our fill of beer!' (Isaiah 56:10, 12). Both of these chapters need to be kept in mind.

The shepherd (verse 2)

'The shepherd' clearly is Jesus Christ.

The watchman (verse 3)

This must be John the Baptist because he did all the things that the Old Testament said would be performed by 'the forerunner' who would announce the Messiah.

The sheep (verse 1)

'Sheep' is a marvellous description of our helplessness and stupidity as God's people. But even though we are 'sheep', once we know Jesus, his voice becomes familiar.

Thieves and robbers (verse 1)

There are those who have climbed into leadership by an unauthorized route ('gate'; verse 1).

The parable applied (verses 7–18)

The gateway to an overflowing life (verse 10)

There is no doubt about the 'gate' in these verses. It is Jesus, and he reinforces the point with the familiar 'I tell you the truth', adding that those who enter by him 'will be saved'. 'Saved' is not a word that John often uses, and here he uses it to mean the ability to live 'life to the full' (verse 10). The life that Jesus gives will be an 'overflowing' experience, when compared with the cramped and restricted offer of the Pharisees.

Thieves and robbers and the hired hand (verses 1, 12–13)

We have already seen that the 'thieves and robbers' (verse 1) had come by an unauthorized way into leadership. Now they are described as those who 'came before me'. Don't imagine that Jesus is thinking about leaders of another generation; it is the present leadership that he has in mind. He goes on to say that in contrast to the 'full' life *he* gives, all that *they* can give is death and destruction (verse 10). Indeed they are like the 'hired hand' who will make no sacrifice for the sheep and who 'cares nothing' for them. If your local library has a book on the paintings in Manchester City art gallery, look at Holman Hunt's *The Hireling*. He painted it to depict the 'hired hand' in these verses. The painting shows a 'hireling' shepherd, his arm around a girl and with a picnic spread in front of them. The sheep, meanwhile, are rampaging through a wheat field in the background and eating unripe corn which will be fatal for them.

The good shepherd (verse 14)

The goodness of Jesus 'the good shepherd' (verse 11) is an attractive goodness. William Temple, a former Archbishop of Canterbury, said it is possible 'to be morally good repulsively'. Jesus is exactly the opposite, and he added the attractive quality of a sacrificial life. He says he will 'lay down his life for the sheep' and amazingly 'take it up again'. He is totally in control of his life; death for this unusual shepherd won't be defeat but victory. How different from the other so-called 'spiritual shepherds' of the day.

An attractive goodness springs from a warm relationship with a holy God and his people. Our goodness will immediately become unattractive once we start to adopt a judgmental or critical spirit. A bitter, negative, gloom-ridden person can never be appealing, no matter how morally upright he might be. Think again of the winsomeness of Jesus and how repulsive the Pharisees were.

Questions

1. What is the main point that Jesus is making with his parable about the sheep and the shepherd? How does this apply to us today?
2. How far are we responsible for each other? How far can we help others before our help becomes unwelcome interference?
3. What contrasts are there between Jesus the good shepherd and his rivals?
4. Should we live for others all the time? How should we decide how much time we need 'to ourselves' to recharge our batteries?

The gate (verse 1)

In these opening verses Jesus is saying something that is very important. Note the formula, 'I tell you the truth'. But in spite of this, it is not immediately clear who or what the 'gate' is. Perhaps it is worth saying that it is dangerous to tie any of these images down too tightly. In general terms in this chapter, Jesus is the 'gate' (verse 7). But in these particular verses (1–3) he is saying that as 'shepherd' he has come in the right way; he has used the 'gate' that the Scriptures said he would.

The word 'sheep pen' actually means courtyard which is the translation used when speaking of that place in the high priest's house (18:15; see also Matthew 26:3; Mark 14:54). It refers to the open space around which most houses were built. It was obviously a safe place to keep your sheep at night and it could be made even more secure by getting a 'watchman' to sleep across the entrance; he would literally become the 'gate'.

One flock (verse 16)

Part of this chapter has left its indelible mark on church history. One old translation says 'there shall be one fold (one sheep pen) and one shepherd' (AV). The translators repeated the mistake originally made by Jerome in the fourth century.

What Jesus said is that there are 'other sheep that are not of this sheep pen'; in other words, God has other people who are not Jewish. But they are all part of the 'one flock' belonging to the 'one shepherd'. There is no suggestion here that there would ever only be 'one sheep pen', in the sense of 'one denomination' or one 'special church', that has God's favour. There is a unity among the 'sheep', not uniformity among the 'sheep pens'.

John 10:19–42

The false shepherds reject the Good Shepherd

Jesus' attack on the Jewish leaders is too much for them and again they resort to violence, the last resort when faith and reason have been abandoned.

Leaders divided

Remember when John uses the phrase 'the Jews' (verses 19, 24, 31) he is not talking about the nation as a whole, but the little group of leaders who were opposed to Jesus. This group is now divided; some are saying that Jesus is 'demon-possessed and raving mad', while others respond, 'These are not the sayings of a man possessed by a demon'. 'The Jews' gather around Jesus and demand, 'How long will you keep us in suspense? If you are the Christ, tell us plainly.' The situation concludes when some 'picked up stones to stone him'. There are several things we need to notice here.

All this takes place in 'Solomon's Colonnade' at the time of 'the Feast of the Dedication'. The roof of the colonnade was supported by arched pillars on four sides providing ample protection against the cold winds of 'winter'. Eventually this was to be one of the first meeting-places of the early Christian believers (Acts 5:12).

Even though the location has changed the subject hasn't. Jesus continues to talk about the shepherds and the flock (verses 26–27). And those who confront him are still the false shepherds who have come to 'kill and destroy' (cf. verses 27–28).

'The Jews' want to be told 'plainly' if Jesus is 'the Christ' (verse 24). They want a straight answer of 'yes' or 'no'. Jesus says that he has told them, but in any case 'the miracles' that he does in his 'Father's name speak for' him. The real problem he says is that 'you are not my sheep'. The 'you' is emphatic; so we have a vivid contrast between those who don't belong to him and those who are '(his) sheep'.

For those who do belong to Jesus, there is eternal security.

- They listen to his voice (verse 27).

- He knows them (verse 27).

- They follow him (verse 27).

- He gives them eternal life (verse 28).

- They will never perish (verse 28).

- No-one can snatch them out of his hand (verse 28).

- They have been given to Jesus by the Father (verse 29).

The fact that the Jews were willing to consider stoning Jesus (verse 31) speaks of the strength of their anger at what they considered 'blasphemy'. But when you ask the question, 'Where did they get the stones from?', the only possible answer is that they had taken them into the temple to throw. Because there certainly wouldn't be any stones just lying around within the sacred precincts. They must have planned to lynch Jesus before they had heard what he said.

Back across the Jordan (verses 40–42)

The hostility of 'the Jews' meant that Jesus had to withdraw from Jerusalem. He headed in a north-easterly direction to the place where John the Baptist 'had been baptising in the early days'. Indeed it was the place where Jesus' own ministry had begun. Note:

▶ 'Many people came to him.'

▶ They recognized that although John hadn't 'performed a miraculous sign', all that he had said about Jesus 'was true'.

▶ As a result, 'many believed in Jesus'.

Questions

1. How would you answer someone who suggested that Jesus is setting out in verse 16 the ideal of a world-wide 'super-church'? Do you think such a thing would work?
2. What is significant about the way Jesus responds to the request for a plain statement about who he is? How far is this relevant to how we talk about him today?
3. What truths about those who belong to Jesus are emphasized by the shepherd/sheep imagery? Apply them to your own situation/church/fellowship.

The Feast of Dedication (verse 22)

'The Feast of Dedication' or 'Feast of Lights' was a relatively new festival in Bible times. It was hardly a century and a half old at the time of Christ. Today it is called 'Hanukkah' and is much like

'Tabernacles'. Sometimes it is even called 'the feast of Tabernacles in the month of Chisleu' (2 Maccabees 1:19).

This feast commemorates the time in 146 BC when Judas
Maccabaeus cleansed and rededicated the temple after its
desecration by Antiochus Epiphanes. The Syrian king captured
Jerusalem in 167 BC and, apart from liking everything Greek, he
seemed to have had an ugly anti-Jewish streak in his make-up.
He changed the worship in the temple to a fertility religion on
Greek lines, with the attendant prostitute-priestesses. He
ordered the daily sacrifices to be offered on an altar to Zeus.
Not surprisingly, Judas Maccabaeus became a national hero
when he recaptured Jerusalem and returned the temple to its
proper use.

John 11:1–16

Jesus allows Lazarus to die

**The friend of Jesus, Lazarus, is reported to be
seriously ill. Jesus, strangely, does nothing and
Lazarus dies.**

Lazarus is dead

The name of the sick man was Lazarus. It
doesn't sound possible in English, but it is the
shortened form of the Old Testament's *Eleazer* meaning 'God is
my help'. Lazarus lived in Bethany with his two sisters Martha
and Mary.

When Jesus heard that Lazarus was ill, he seemed to be
certain that the final outcome would not be death and that

somehow it would result in God's glory. Yet surprisingly 'he stayed where he was two more days' (verse 6). In normal circumstances we would have expected him to rush to his friend's side. It has been suggested that the delay was to make certain that Lazarus was dead because Jesus wanted to 'raise' him and not merely heal him. However, that doesn't take into account what the passage is saying. Lazarus was dead before the message arrived; yet somehow Jesus knew the final outcome would not be death.

Day and night

'Are there not twelve hours of daylight?' (verse 9) seems to be straightforward enough, as does 'A man who walks by day will not stumble'. But Jewish days and nights were a little more complicated than ours. It is true that there were twelve hours in a day and the same number at night. But because there was more daylight in the summer, each daylight 'hour' was longer to cover the extra amount of light. At night in the summer the 'hours' were correspondingly shorter. 'Twelve hours' was simply a way of referring to a whole day. That is what Jesus is saying here, implying that there is always enough time to do what has to be done.

'Sleep' and 'death'

Jesus says, 'Our friend Lazarus has fallen asleep' (verse 11) and he was 'speaking of his death'. 'Has fallen asleep' is a characteristically New Testament way of referring to the death of a believer, but it presents problems.

Before Christ came, death was man's great enemy and in the ancient world it was universally feared. It seemed to be an enemy that couldn't be defeated, but the resurrection of Jesus changed that. By saying that Lazarus was 'asleep', Jesus could simply be taking the 'sting' out of death and telling Martha that this was a natural way for a believer to step from one world into the next. Paul uses the same idea and speaks of 'those who have fallen asleep' (1 Corinthians 15:20). The idea is underlined in our culture by the word 'cemetery' which means 'sleeping places'.

The New Testament, however, says that the believer will enjoy an immediate experience of heaven after death; Jesus said to the penitent thief, 'Today you will be with me in paradise' (Luke 23:43).

If the idea of 'sleep' poses a problem, then the idea of a 'bodiless soul' creates even more. Perhaps 'sleep' is the best way of describing death from the point of view of time because the same event viewed from eternity could be an immediate experience of heaven. It would be possible for two people to die ten million years apart and yet for both to step into eternity at precisely the same moment, because eternity is not restricted by time.

Questions

1. Why did Jesus delay before setting out in response to the news about Lazarus? How does this help us in understanding delays in answers to our prayers?
2. What problems are there with describing death as 'being asleep'? How may these be resolved?
3. Pool what you know about how different cultures/religions have approached the problem of death. Which is the most helpful and why?

Doubts about this miracle

John is the only gospel writer to include this miracle and some have suggested therefore that it didn't really take place. The doubters argue that it happened so close to Jerusalem, was seen by such a large crowd, and was so important a miracle that other writers would have included it if it were true. But one or two things need to be said:

▶ We can't be certain that the other writers had heard about it. Peter wasn't there and he was normally Mark's source. Matthew is following Mark's order of events at this point (cf. Matthew 19:3 – 20:34; 26:6–13; Mark 10:2–52; 14:3–9). It could be argued that Peter was absent from all the events of this time and didn't rejoin the disciples until just before the Passover. He is not mentioned by John (6:69 – 13:6); nor is he found in Matthew (19:27 – 26:33) and he is nowhere to be seen in Luke (18:28 – 22:8).

▶ A miracle of 'resurrection' wasn't necessarily as important then as it is for us. The ancient world was full of unusual epics. Even Luke doesn't put the raising of the widow's son in a prominent place and that was a similar miracle of resurrection power.

▶ John's gospel is different from the other three. For seventy years John had time to think over the events in the life of Christ, and was able to read what the others had written. He seems to have deliberately chosen not to repeat some detail and to flesh out the narrative where he thought something was missing. The raising of Lazarus was such an event. Note the present tense (verse 7); John was there.

John 11:17–57

The resurrection and the life

Jesus' dramatic restoration of Lazarus to life is a sign that 'Resurrection' is, as it were, Jesus' second name. He *is* everlasting life for all.

According to Jewish belief the 'soul' of a departed person remained near the body for four days and then left the vicinity completely. So when John says that the body of Lazarus had already been in the tomb for four days he is saying that he was completely dead and totally beyond help.

The proximity of Bethany to Jerusalem meant that 'many Jews had come' to pay their respects. The first week after Lazarus' death would be a time of deep mourning, so note that 'the Jews' didn't call simply to commiserate and assure the family of their prayers; they had come to participate fully in the mourning (verse 19).

A woman of faith (verses 17–27)

It was typical of these two sisters that when they heard that Jesus was coming, Martha hurried to meet him while Mary stayed at home. Martha confides that she knows that God will do whatever Jesus asks, but adds with a tinge of regret, 'Lord, if you had been here, my brother would not have died.' Jesus assures her of Lazarus' resurrection, which Martha takes to be a reference to 'the last day'. He counters with one of the great declarations of the fourth gospel, 'I am the resurrection and the life' (verse 25). Jesus adds the pronoun to the verb as we have seen before. He says, 'I–I am the resurrection and the life.'

Surprisingly, 'resurrection' is hardly mentioned in this gospel (the only other place is in 5:29), but 'life' is a major theme. Jesus *is* both the resurrection *and* the life. Note Jesus isn't one and gives the other; he *is* both. The result is that 'he who believes in (him) will live, even though he dies; and whoever lives and believes in (him) will never die' (verse 26). In response Martha says she believes Jesus to be the 'Christ, the Son of God'. In other words she recognized him to be the Messiah.

At the grave-side (verses 28–37)

Martha called to Mary, 'The teacher is here'. As Mary goes to meet him, 'the Jews' who had been with her presumed she had hurried off to the tomb 'to mourn' (verse 31). For us in the twentieth century, it sounds as if she has gone to the grave for a few quiet moments. But that could not be further from the truth; the word 'mourn' means 'a loud painful expression of sadness'. It is telling us about funerals in Bible times, which were similar to those in most parts of the Middle East today. You might have caught a glimpse of one on the television news. Mary's initial reaction to Jesus is virtually the same as Martha's (verse 32; cf. verse 21).

Lazarus walks out of the grave (verses 38–44)

The scene moves to the mouth of the 'cave' where the body of Lazarus had been interred, with Jesus asking for the 'stone laid across the entrance' (verse 38) to be taken away. There is a mild protest from Martha who can only think of the unpleasant side of opening a grave. Jesus reminds her of what he has already said (verse 40). There is a problem here because Martha wasn't present earlier to hear what was said when Jesus spoke about God's glory (verse 4). Jesus prays and calls to Lazarus, literally, 'Lazarus, come here, outside'. Because of the grave clothes Lazarus can only hobble out. Jesus commands that these be untied and Lazarus released. There is so much detail here, we can only be reading the words of an eye-witness.

For the believer, the full horror of death that had gripped the ancient world is removed in an instant. To know that Jesus is the life-force at work behind the universe (John 1) is encouraging. To be told that we can be 'born again' (John 3) adds comfort. But finally, to be given facts that demonstrate that death is powerless before Jesus must be the crowning assurance for the believer.

The plot to kill Jesus (verses 45–53)

Giving life back to Lazarus had two results.

▶ Some 'put their faith in' Jesus.

▶ The chief priests and the Pharisees 'called a meeting of the Sanhedrin', the Jewish parliament, the result of which was that 'Caiaphas, who was high priest that year' declared, 'It is better for . . . one man to die for the people than that the whole nation perish' (verse 50). His cynical solution had a deeper meaning than he realized; indeed John calls it a prophecy. Now they plot to take Jesus' life (verse 53).

It is not possible to identify 'Ephraim' (verse 54) with any certainty, but most think it is *El-Tayibeth*, about fifteen miles from Jerusalem. It was secure enough for Jesus to escape arrest but also close enough for him to go to Jerusalem when he was ready.

Questions

1. How would you answer someone who suggested that the silence of the other gospels at this point means that John must have made up the story?
2. In what way is this event 'the crowning assurance for the believer'?
3. What repercussions were there following this incident? How

do you react when tempted to avoid doing what is right in order to avoid unpleasant consequences?

'Deeply moved'

'Deeply moved' (verse 33) is difficult to translate. James Moffat's translation reads 'Jesus *chafed* in spirit'; E. V. Rieu says that Jesus 'gave way to such *distress of spirit* as made his body tremble'. In a recent translation Eugene Peterson renders it, 'a *deep anger* welled up within him'. In classical Greek it is used of a horse *snorting*. John uses the same word again almost immediately (verse 38) and in both cases he seems to suggest that Jesus gave an indignant snort at the ultimate devastation that sin had brought into the life of his friend (Romans 6:23).

John 12:1–11

A family dinner party

Foot-washing was a normal courtesy at a dinner party but Mary's extravagance was exceptional. Hints of betrayal and death begin to creep into the narrative.

The loving worship of Mary

The final storm over the ministry of Jesus was about to break. There was just time for him to make one last visit to his friends at Bethany and in the warm family atmosphere he prepares for the darkest week of his life.

131

Note that Lazarus was there. You can imagine him recalling the events of the last chapter from his point of view.

Two of the other gospel writers tell us that the house where the dinner was given in Jesus' honour was the home of 'Simon the Leper' (Matthew 26:6; Mark 14:3). It is quite possible, therefore, that Mary, Martha and Lazarus were Simon's children. One thing we must not do is to confuse the story with the account of the woman Luke describes as 'a sinner' (Luke 7:37), nor must we mix up 'Simon the Leper' with 'Simon the Pharisee' (Luke 7:39–40), who were clearly two different people.

In these verses two things are contrasted.

▶ The loving worship of Mary. 'Worship' means 'giving worth' and that is what Mary was doing by taking a 'pint of pure nard' and anointing the feet of Jesus before wiping them with her hair.

▶ The objecting meanness of Judas (verses 4, 6). John makes it clear that Judas wasn't really interested in the poor, simply the availability of cash to steal.

Jesus says Mary was to be left alone (verse 7) which is an indication that he thought no-one should criticize what she has done; the 'scented oil' was hers to use as she wished. What is intriguing about the reply is that Jesus links the perfume with his burial. Maybe Mary didn't fully understand the implications of her actions. Perhaps she just felt that Jesus' life was coming to an end and she wanted to celebrate it. Smell can be so evocative, and John's memory is triggered as he recalls that 'the house was filled with the fragrance of the perfume'.

An expensive perfume

Mary anointed the feet of Jesus with 300 gms of a very expensive scented oil. The older translations called it an 'ointment' while the newer ones suggest 'perfume', but it was neither 'smeared' nor 'dabbed on', it was 'poured' (verse 3). The scent could have come from the stems of the tiny pink and white flowers of the valerian family, *Nardostachys Jatamansi* to give it its botanical name, which came from India. In Bible times, traders came from the East to sell spices and perfumes.

The box where the money was kept

The word for 'money-bag' (verse 6; 13:29) is quite unusual and describes a money-box. Originally it was used of the little box in which a musician kept the mouthpiece of his flute. John is the only one to hint before the betrayal that there was possibly something morally wrong with Judas. Perhaps Judas was able to cover up the evidence of his avarice and it was only with hindsight that John was able to see the clues that had always been there.

Questions

---

1. What contrasts between Mary and Judas does this passage highlight? How can they help us to live better lives?
2. In what ways can we today show self-giving love in our worship?
3. Does the way we demonstrate that love depend on our personalities? Discuss different degrees of display of feelings and what each group member is comfortable with.

Meals in the ancient world

'Dinner' (verse 2) was the one meal of the day that was special in the ancient world. The diners would linger over it, enjoying it to the full as it bound them together: host, guests, friends and family.

- *Breakfast* would consist of yesterday's dry bread softened with wine.

- *Lunch* would be an *al fresco* meal taken in the field, market-place or wherever you happened to be.

- *Dinner* or *Supper* was unhurried and leisurely and consisted of much more than food and drink. There was unlimited time to enjoy the meal and the company. Remember that it was a 'supper' that Jesus used to illustrate his relationship with the believer (Revelation 3:20).

John 12:12–19

Jesus rides into Jerusalem

Great crowds gather to see this prophet who can even raise the dead.

The triumphal entry into Jerusalem

We have already noticed that it was compulsory for all adult Jewish men to attend the Passover, and that all Jewish men who lived anywhere in the Roman Empire would try to be at the Feast at least once in a lifetime. So Jerusalem was packed with a 'great crowd' and the atmosphere was explosive. When they discovered 'that Jesus was on his way', the crowd 'took palm branches and went out to meet him, shouting, "Hosanna!".' Jesus responded by finding a young donkey and sitting on him.

Reactions to Jesus

▶ Some were merely sightseers; they had heard a rumour that someone had been raised from the dead and they wanted to catch sight of the miracle worker (verse 18).

▶ Others had seen Jesus raise Lazarus and were convinced that he was the Messiah. Some of these would know the prophecy in Zechariah 9:9 (verse 15) so they might well have led the palm-scattering and the shouting of 'Hosanna' (verse 13).

▶ Also in the group were antagonistic Pharisees who said to each other, 'See, this is getting us nowhere. Look how the whole world has gone after him' (verse 19).

▶ There was a group of disciples who were committed to Jesus but only with hindsight understood the details of the events (verse 16).

▶ Finally there was a small group of foreigners (verse 20), but more about them in the next section.

'Hosanna!'

The crowd cried, 'Hosanna!' (verse 13). Here is a marvellous word that has become part of the English language and is especially used around Easter, so it is surprising that we don't actually know what it means.

It is a transliteration of the Hebrew from Psalm 118:25 (English letters have been substituted for Hebrew) and it is normally rendered, 'O LORD, save us . . .' But this raises the question of why was a cry for deliverance used when the crowd was welcoming their Messiah? If everybody had got on their knees and said, 'Save us, O Lord' it would have made much more sense; but to stand and cheer doesn't fit the interpretation.

Augustine said it suggested 'a state of mind, rather than

135

having any positive significance'. In other words, it was like the English 'Hooray' which one dictionary mysteriously defines as a 'later substitute for Huzza', without telling us what 'Huzza' means!

Questions

---

1. How did people behave when Jesus entered Jerusalem on a donkey? What led to these reactions? What kind of reactions to Jesus do we find today?
2. It is easy to shout 'Hosanna', even when we do not know what it means. But how can we ensure that our worship is more than the excitement of feeling?
3. Jesus came in peace, but his followers have often made war. Is there such a thing as a 'just war'? How could we justify it?

Jesus rides on a young donkey

At the end of the 20th century, the idea of Jesus riding into Jerusalem on a 'young donkey' (verse 14) is a charming picture that would make a good illustration for a children's Bible, but it probably isn't something we would like to share with our friends at work or down at the pub. If we say that, we are missing a very powerful piece of Hebrew imagery. When a king went to war he rode a horse; if he wanted to show that he came in peace he would ride a donkey. So, when Mephibosheth went to see David he rode on a donkey (2 Samuel 19:26) as did Ahithophel (2 Samuel 17:23). When the Old Testament tells us that Jair had 'thirty sons who rode thirty donkeys' (Judges 10:4) we are being told that they were peaceful guardians in the 'thirty towns' of Gilead.

John 12:20–36

Jesus predicts his death

The idea that death could be the culmination of Jesus' glorious ministry is unthinkable to the disciples and to the crowd. Yet this is Jesus' theme.

The Greeks

John is the only gospel writer to mention the 'Greeks' (verse 20) who had come and asked for an interview with Jesus. All we know about them is that they had come 'to worship at the Feast'. With a whole Pantheon of 'gods' who behaved as badly as human beings, it is not surprising that few serious-minded Greeks were attracted to the God of the Bible. But whether they were 'proselytes' who had been fully converted to Judaism or merely 'God-fearers' we don't know. If they had stood in the right place in Jerusalem they could have seen Jesus, but they were really asking for more than that. They wanted to talk to Jesus and get to know his teaching.

Jesus speaks plainly

We have noticed several times that Jesus did not think the time was right (2:4; 7:6, 8); now notice his statement, 'The hour has come for the Son of Man to be glorified' (verse 23) and he adds the formula, 'I tell you the truth'. Jesus has several important things to say about his death.

▶ 'Unless a grain of wheat falls to the ground' (verse 24). Jesus says that the only fruitful way to live always involves death. The seed must 'die' in the ground if the new plant is to emerge. He asks his disciples to follow his example; he wants them to die to their old way of life so that the totally new life can emerge. He warns them that he 'who loves his life will lose it, while the man who hates his life . . . will keep it for eternal life'.

▶ 'For this very reason I came to this hour' (verse 27). Jesus is agitated: 'my heart is troubled.' It is a very strong verb speaking of something that is more than mildly disturbing. The other writers tell us about Gethsemane. Jesus sees his death approaching and although part of him shrinks from it, he sees that his whole life has been leading to this moment.

▶ 'But I, when I am lifted up' (verses 32, 34). This is the third time that Jesus has spoken about being 'lifted up' (3:14; 8:28). It is not the usual way of referring to crucifixion, but we know what he means. John could well be pointing his readers to another aspect; the fact that one day Jesus will be 'lifted up' above everything else. Indeed 'exaltation' is so much the idea behind these words that, to avoid any misunderstanding, John feels he must add, 'He said this to show the kind of death he was going to die' (verse 33).

▶ 'You are going to have the light just a little while longer' (verse 35). 'Light', of course, is one of the great themes of this gospel and Jesus returns to it after the people have misunderstood what the Bible says about the 'Son of Man'. Here 'light' is used as a warning. They are to learn to 'walk while (they) have the light' before it is taken from them. They are to 'put (their) trust in the light' and 'become sons of light' before 'the darkness overtakes' them.

Questions

1. 'We would like to see Jesus' (verse 21). Discuss the possible degrees of commitment implied; curiosity, thirst for knowl-

edge, acquaintance, dedication . . . How can we help people from one stage to the next?

2. What does it mean in practice for you to 'die to (your) old way of life so that the totally new life can emerge'?

3. In what ways has Jesus brought 'light' into the world? How would you explain the idea to an unbeliever who sees Jesus as bringing 'darkness'?

John 12:37–50

Blind unbelief

In spite of a mighty miracle and a triumphal entry into Jerusalem, not everyone accepted Jesus. John shows that Isaiah predicted this. The section concludes with the final words of Jesus spoken in public.

Unbelief predicted (verses 37–41)

John gives us two passages from Isaiah showing that hundreds of years before his birth, it was predicted that not everyone would accept the Messiah. The first quotation comes from chapter 53, part of one of the *Songs of the suffering servant*, which says that the humanness of the incarnation would hide the Messiah from many (Isaiah 53:1, 3).

The second passage is saying the same thing (Isaiah 6:9–10), but is a little more difficult. The second quotation comes from Isaiah's commissioning as a prophet. At this time he was told that his hearers would be totally (eyes, ears and heart) unable to understand what he was saying. Alec Motyer says that the prophecy of Isaiah bears 'all the marks of a plain, systematic, reasoned approach' (*The Prophecy of Isaiah*, IVP, 1993, p. 79), yet his hearers rejected it. The criticism levelled at Isaiah in his generation (Isaiah 28:9–10) was that he taught with such a simplicity and clarity of style that the sophisticates of his day rejected him. He didn't sound profound or deep enough for them. The point that John is making is that what was true of Isaiah was also true of Jesus. Clearly Jesus had a very plain, systematic (and) reasoned approach too. Verse 40 is important because it is quoted in each of the first six books of the New Testament. Every time it is saying that the good news of God's kingdom is plain to those who accept it, but those who set themselves against this good news find that they are hardened by it, just as people were in Isaiah's day.

Secret disciples (verses 42–43)

Not all that Jesus said fell on deaf ears: 'Many even among the leaders believed in him.' But this group was unwilling to confess their faith openly because of the Pharisees and for fear of excommunication. The reason that John gives for their secret discipleship must be among the saddest words in the New Testament: 'they loved praise from men more than praise from God'. Before you think too badly of them, imagine living in a country with an extremely fundamentalist Muslim culture; such places are still producing martyrs today. Even if we live in a place where no pressures exist there is still a principle to be learned, and it is that we must live in the light of eternity rather than time.

Inescapable judgment (verses 44–50)

These are the final words that Jesus will speak to the public at large. In essence they contain the idea that is behind his whole life and ministry. Jesus claims that when men and women are confronted by him, they are in fact confronted by God. His words are God's words and to reject them will incur God's judgment on 'the last day' (verse 48). As always in this gospel, the emphasis is on what 'leads to eternal life', because Jesus 'has come into the world as a light' so that those who believe him should not 'stay in darkness'.

Questions

1. Think of a situation in the past where you should have been open about your allegiance to Jesus, but in fact hid it? What can you learn from it?
2. What wrong reactions would 'harden my heart' against the Kingdom of God and how should I avoid them?
3. Is the Scripture really telling us that the more plainly we speak about God, the less people will understand? Or the more accurately and simply we present God, the more they want to run away from him? How does their dilemma guide us in our witness and evangelism?

JESUS SAYS 'GOODBYE' TO HIS FRIENDS

John 13:1 – 17:26

John 13:1–17

The servant Jesus

Jesus turns the master/disciple relationship upside down by taking a towel and washing his disciple's feet, an example of self-sacrificing love.

The stage is set for the final drama. 'Jesus knew that the time had come for him to leave this world' and, while the supper was being served, he was aware that Judas had slipped out to betray him. At first, when you focus on what happened here, it is all rather ordinary. They were enjoying a meal together when Jesus left the table, as if he was about to tackle a household chore. He 'took off his outer clothing, and wrapped a towel round his waist' (verse 4). It was only when he started to wash his disciples' feet that the scene became incongruous. Traditionally it should have happened the other way around with the disciples washing his feet.

Footwashing in perspective

The love Jesus had for his disciples

So far (chapters 1–12), John has used the noun 'love' and the verb 'to love' nine times. In this section (John 12:1 – 17:26) he will use them thirty times. And it is at the cross that Jesus will show 'the full extent of his love' (verse 1). Here, as if he is preparing his disciples, he washes their feet.

The need to be made spiritually clean

Nothing was said until Jesus reached Peter who was very upset by what Jesus was doing: 'You shall never wash my feet.' Jesus answered, 'Unless I wash you, you have no part with me.' Peter then goes to the other extreme: 'Not just my feet but my hands and my head as well!' What Jesus said here is true for every disciple. We can have no part in the Kingdom of God until Jesus has made us spiritually clean. 'Salvation' or being 'born again' (John 3:3) are all ways of describing this spiritual 'washing'.

There is a lesson that must be learnt by all disciples: 'I have set you an example that you should do as I have done . . . no servant is greater than his master' (verses 15–16). This isn't an optional extra; every disciple is to serve others.

Learning to be a servant

Recently at a conference I was on the team speaking to leaders. On the last day we held a clinic to deal with questions. One of the team was asked the most important lesson he had learnt about ministry. After a pause he spoke about something that had happened years ago. Just after his conversion he was asked to help at a summer camp. He had been appointed health officer for the camp and imagined he would walk around all day in a white coat with a stethoscope around his neck. In reality he was asked to dig holes for the latrines and to surround them with a hessian screen. He was then instructed to get up early each morning and scrub the wooden lavatory seats with boiling water and disinfectant.

On the first morning, armed with a bucket, he prepared to set about his task, when he discovered someone had had an accident in the night. In disgust he left the job undone, but later in the day he saw the camp's leader doing it. And the leader did it every morning without any further comment. 'That was the most important lesson I ever learnt about ministry,' he said and added, 'Ministry and leadership is about service, not authority.' It is a sacrificial love that is expected from all involved.

Questions

1. What truths about Jesus does this footwashing incident highlight for the disciples? How do they apply to us?
2. What are contemporary equivalents to footwashing? Is there sometimes value in literally washing each others' feet?
3. In what ways have you experienced the truth that ministry 'is about service not authority'? Where does the power of God come in?

Footwashing in history

Footwashing was quickly taken up by the early church and sadly formalized. What the Queen does on Maundy Thursday is all that remains, in a highly ritualized form, for us. Next time you see it on television note that although there is no footwashing today, the officials still wear white towel aprons and the Queen carries a nosegay, a medieval air-freshener, to disguise the odour of the feet.

It was the Synod of Toledo in AD 694 that made footwashing obligatory for the church on Maundy Thursday. In 1530 Cardinal Wolsey washed and kissed the feet of fifty-nine poor men at Peterborough. In 1213, King John started the tradition of the royal family washing the feet of the poor. He washed the feet of thirteen men at Rochester and gave each of them thirteen pence. These coins have become known as Royal Maundy, or Maundy money.

The word 'Maundy' comes from the Latin 'mandatum' referring to the new commandment or 'mandate' of love (verse 34).

John 13:18–38

God's love-plan unfolds

Jesus looks into the future to his betrayal and death, seeing them as avenues to God's glory and his disciples' love for one another.

Jesus predicts his betrayal (verses 18–30)

Not one of the disciples emerges from the events surrounding the death of Jesus unscathed. At the critical moment they all abandoned him (Mark 14:50). But none failed so disastrously as Judas.

Jesus was 'troubled in spirit' (verse 21). We have already met this word (11:33; 12:27) and we need to notice here the deep emotional upheaval that took place as he faced the cost of going to the cross. In this chapter he was troubled because one of the disciples was about 'to betray' him. We aren't told specifically who it was. John was writing from hindsight and has already told us that it was Judas Iscariot (verse 2), prompted by the devil. But, at the time, the disciples were at a loss to know who it would be. The New Testament doesn't give us a full account of Judas and his motives. We are told that he was dishonest, and that possibly played a part in the betrayal, but it can't have been the whole story.

Several times one of the disciples was described as the one

'whom Jesus loved' (verse 23; 19:26; 21:7, 20), but again we are not told who it was; he is never named. Some think it was Lazarus because we are told that Jesus loved him (11:3, 5, 36), but it is difficult to see Lazarus in the fishing party at the end of the gospel (21:2). It wasn't Peter, because in these verses he 'motioned' to whoever it was (verse 24). Most probably it was John, modestly referring to himself.

We have already seen that the devil had prompted Judas to betray Jesus. He now 'entered' Judas (verse 27) so the deed could be done. We need to note that the betrayal was the work of a sinful man in co-operation with the devil. Jesus tells Judas to hurry up with what he has to do. 'And it was night', says John dramatically; all he could remember was the impenetrable darkness of the event.

The new commandment (verses 31–33)

John, as we have already noticed, sometimes used the word 'glorify' to speak about the death of Christ (p. 137). In these verses he now uses the word in its usual sense of being 'invested with the radiance of heaven'. Jesus is about to die and this will mean that Father and Son will be made glorious in heaven. Jesus tells his disciples that he will be with them only a little longer, and that where he is going to they can't come at the moment. Note:

Aspects of love

Jesus gives his disciples 'a new commandment' (verse 34). This is the only time in John's gospel that Jesus uses this particular word 'new'. There is another word that means 'recent in time', in the sense that it hasn't been seen before. But the word here means 'fresh', in the sense of quality. The commandment to 'love one another' is as old as the beginning of the Old Testament (Leviticus 19:18), but Jesus is giving it a fresh quality. The disciples must love one another as *he has loved them*. That is to be the new aspect of their love.

Peter's response

Jesus has already told the disciples he will only be with them a little longer and that they won't be able to follow him. But Peter wants to come straight away. Sadly, Jesus had to tell him that he would 'disown (him) three times' (verse 38) before the cock crows. So a section that begins with the sacrificial love of Jesus for his disciples concludes with the possibility of them being disloyal to him.

Questions

1. How would you answer someone who suggested that the devil, rather than Judas, was responsible for the betrayal of Jesus? How does your answer affect us today?
2. Peter is often impulsive in his action. Is it better to act on impulse or always to think and pray things over before doing anything? Share examples.
3. What is *new* about the 'new commandment' that Jesus gives his disciples?

Seating arrangement for meals

We won't be able to visualize the scene properly until we have a few more details about the seating arrangements for the evening meal. Strictly speaking, the guests weren't seated at all – they reclined. We see this happening here because John was 'leaning back against' Jesus (verse 25). The table would be very low, just a few inches off the ground and surrounded by couches of a similar height, called *trilinias*, each holding up to three people. The guests would recline on their left elbows and use their right hand for eating. Apart from the person at the back of the couch there would be a slight overlapping, with the other two able to lean back against someone else.

John 14:1–14

Jesus, the only way

Jesus gives us a brief glimpse of heaven and makes a staggering claim – he is the only way in.

A vision of rest and refreshment

We must be careful not to have a *House & Garden* magazine image in our minds when we interpret, 'In my Father's house are many rooms'. B. F. Westcott starts to take us back to the biblical picture when he says that the rooms were 'lodging places' on a road, where a weary traveller would find rest and refreshment. Archbishop William Temple says the word means 'a wayside caravanserai', a hotel for merchants who travelled the trading routes of the ancient world. A 'caravanserai' would consist of a single building where the proprietor lived with his family. The main feature would be ample space for several camel caravans to come for rest, with a good supply of water for the animals and a large area where tents could be pitched. If the caravanserai was in a desert it would have the atmosphere of an oasis, with trees providing shade from the sun. At night, when all the guests had arrived and the animals had been settled and made secure, there would be feasting well into the night. A caravan's progress across the desert could be hindered by slipping loads and escaping children, so the prospect of a caravanserai would be eagerly awaited by the weary travellers. However, this vision of rest and refreshment could be dulled by the possibility of a 'no vacancies' sign at the end of the journey. To ensure that this didn't happen, the caravan master would send his servant on ahead to book the required number of places. Jesus indicates that he will do the same: 'I am going there to prepare a place for you' (verse 2).

Not all roads lead to heaven

With so much detail it is surprising that the disciples want still more information. Perhaps it needed a doubter such as Thomas to point to the flaw in the argument. So having discovered that heaven is as real as a place on a map, the disciples are now told that Jesus is the road on the map ('the way'), and the right direction down it ('the truth'), and even the motive power ('the life') along it (verse 6). All this is getting a little too deep for Philip: 'Lord, show us the Father and that will be enough for us.' It is possible that Philip thought that instead of teaching in parables, a new vision of God was all that was necessary. The word 'enough' is the same word that he had used at the feeding of the five thousand ('eight months' wages would not buy *enough* bread', 6:7). The underlying truth of the whole gospel is summarized in a single sentence, 'Anyone who has seen me has seen the Father.'

Questions

1. What do these verses teach us about heaven?
2. What is so disappointing about Philip's question here? Share in your group what kind of evidence you would like. What would be 'enough' for you (verse 8)?

Works and greater works

We have already seen that the word that John uses for 'miracles' indicates that they were significant events: 'signs' (2:11). But Jesus often uses the word 'work' to describe them (verses 10–11). There was a harmonious mixture of the miraculous and the non-miraculous in the life of Christ. He doesn't distinguish between the two; they were both 'work' for him. Notice, however, that in these verses he doesn't call it his work, but the work that the Father, who was living in him, was doing (verse 10).

We now have a remarkable statement. Note the formula, 'I tell you the truth' (verse 12), warning us that something important is coming: 'anyone who has faith in me will do what I have been doing. He will do even greater things than these (literally 'greater works'), because I am going to the Father.' Whatever these 'greater things' are, they must include the miraculous and the non-miraculous, because we've seen that is how Jesus uses the word. So what are they?

It would be easy to point to the healing miracles of Jesus, but they only brought temporary relief. A miracle which healed the physical body would only last as long as that body. You can put the work of Christ on earth into two categories.

- He healed the sick; giving physical relief in his life.

- He also sought to bring people to the place where they could start enjoying 'the life of God's age' (p. 57) – an experience that was eternal and would last for ever.

So the 'greater things' that the disciples could do must be in the area that touches the eternal; the spiritual rather than the physical. Whatever Jesus did can now be multiplied by the number of disciples. There was only one of him, but there were eleven of them. The sheer quantity of the 'work' that an ever-growing church could do would be colossal. This must be the 'greater things' that Jesus talks about here.

Jesus' exclusive claim

Christianity is the only religion in the world which rests on the person of its founder. That immediately makes Christianity different from the other world religions. Then when you focus on some of the things Jesus said, such as above, you are driven to the conclusion that Jesus was either who he claimed to be, or he was the most outrageous madman the world has ever seen. C. S. Lewis summed it up exactly when he said, 'The discrepancy between the depth, sincerity, and may I say, the shrewdness of his moral teaching, and the rampant megalomania which must lie behind his theological teaching unless he is God has never been got over.' Well, the depth, sincerity and shrewdness of his teaching couldn't be put more clearly than by John in this gospel and, remember, he is not writing about someone he has merely read about. As he puts it elsewhere: that 'which we have heard, which we have seen with our eyes, which we have looked at and our hands have touched – this we proclaim' (1 John 1:1).

Help from on high

Jesus will return to the Father and send the Holy Spirit in his place. At the same time he stresses the link between love and obedience.

Love and the commandments

Some people today would emphasize the need for 'love' at the expense of obedience and the need to keep the commandments. But in a relationship where 'love' is really involved there will be the desire to please the loved one. 'If you love me, you will obey what I command' (verse 15). He later adds, 'If anyone loves me, he will obey my teaching' (verse 23). Obedience will bring the bonus that 'My Father will love him, and we will come to him and make our home with him' (verse 23).

The disciples need not feel abandoned

As a group the disciples would be a close-knit family and Jesus knew that without him they would feel orphaned and abandoned. Leaderless, they would feel as lost as children without parents, so Jesus promises to 'come to' them (verse 18). This seems to refer to his coming in the person of the Holy Spirit, but it could refer to the post-resurrection appearances. The fact that Jesus is going away should not cause the disciples' hearts to be troubled or afraid because, 'Peace I leave with you; my peace I give you' (verse 27). It is interesting that this won't be peace 'as the world gives'. Today 'the world' normally uses the idea of peace in a negative sense. We say that there is peace in Northern

Ireland or Bosnia, when all we mean is that a shot hasn't been fired. Or we say we've had a peaceful day in the office if there weren't many interruptions or telephone calls.

Sometimes the Bible uses the word 'peace' in this way; but it also has a special meaning. It means such spiritual satisfaction, physical well-being and mental tranquillity, that even the possibility of war, strife, and animosity is completely forgotten. No wonder Helmut Thielicke said that it was 'not dull stagnation, but is a soaring, stirring, happy thing' (*The Waiting Father*, James Clarke, 1960, p. 26). That is the sort of peace that Jesus gives to his disciples.

Jesus approaches the end of his earthly life and ministry

You can see the concern of Jesus for his disciples because he told them what was going to happen before it did. He told them, so that when it happened they would believe (verse 29).

As the time for the crucifixion drew near Jesus would not have time to speak to them much longer because, he warned, 'the prince of this world is coming' (verse 30). John is speaking of the devil who wants to blind the world to the reality of Jesus (2 Corinthians 4:4). Jesus must defeat the devil, just as the devil would defeat him if he could; but he couldn't because, as Jesus said, 'he has no hold on me'. Jesus is sinless; so there is no way that the devil could hold him.

The crucifixion would shock the disciples, but in the end they would see it as the victory of Jesus over sin and death; and then they would see it as a demonstration of the love Jesus had for the Father (verse 31).

Questions

_____

1. What does Jesus mean by 'greater things' in verse 12? Do you see them happening today?

2. How would you respond to someone who suggested that as long as we love others, we don't need to bother about rules and regulations?
3. What differences are there between the peace that comes from Jesus and peace 'as the world gives'?

The Father's gift of the Holy Spirit

There is a strong emphasis on the Holy Spirit in the rest of this gospel, whereas little has been said about him so far. There are at least four things we need to notice about the Father's gift of the Spirit.

He is *another* counsellor

When we use the word 'another' we mean something that is quite different. But the word Jesus used means 'something that is separate, but of exactly the same kind'. So when Jesus says, 'I will ask the Father, and he will give you another Counsellor' (verse 16) the implication is that he will be someone very much like Jesus. Indeed elsewhere he is called 'the Spirit of Christ' (Romans 8:9).

He is another *Counsellor*

We have weakened the word 'counsellor' today. Sometimes when we use it, we mean no more than someone who will sympathize with us. But the word Jesus used is a strong one. Perhaps 'strengthener' would be better, because it means someone 'called alongside to help'. It was sometimes used of the person called to help the accused in a Court of Law: the counsel for the defence or the 'advocate' (see 1 John 2:1). John Wycliffe gave us the old translation 'Comforter' which has come to mean something 'soft', while in his day it meant to 'make someone stronger'.

157

He is the *Spirit of truth*

The Spirit can come to help the disciples and make them stronger, but the world 'cannot' receive him. This incompatibility is because the world has shut itself off from spiritual things. How different for the disciples: the Spirit lives with them and will be in them (verse 17). Jesus has just told his disciples that he is 'the truth' (14:6), so it is not surprising that the Spirit whom the Father sends will be 'the Spirit of truth'.

He is the *Holy Spirit*

Our age would want to characterize the Spirit as 'the Giver of mighty gifts' or the 'Exciting Spirit' and it is true that the Holy Spirit's work is exciting and that he does provide many gifts to the church. But the New Testament normally speaks of him, as Jesus does here, as the 'Holy Spirit' (verse 26). It is his character that is important. Notice:

- the Father will send him;

- in the 'name' of the Son;

- to teach the disciples 'all things'; and

- to remind them of 'everything' that Jesus had said.

That last point is important because our age is marked by a perpetual quest for something new. So notice that it is the teaching of Christ ('everything' that Jesus had 'said') that will be the basis of the disciples' understanding and teaching.

There are so many ways to communicate today: the post, the telephone, fax and e-mail. Our messages are carried in hundreds of different ways: by van, truck, aeroplane, cable, radio and satellite. The basic blocks of communication, however, haven't changed; we still use words. Neither has the basic block of Christian truth in God's Word (the Bible) changed. 'New' is not necessarily 'better'.

Questions

1. What does Jesus mean when he promises the arrival of 'another' Counsellor?
2. What does the word translated 'Counsellor' really mean? In what ways have you found the Holy Spirit doing this?
3. Why does the New Testament emphasize that he is the 'Holy' Spirit? What does this imply for us?

John 15:1–8

The vine and its fruit

Jesus uses a vine as a powerful illustration of the relationship between himself, the Father and the disciples. As in nature, so in spiritual life, pruning produces abundant fruit.

Jesus and his disciples were still in the upper room and he had just said to them, 'Come now; let us leave' (14:31). Surprisingly nobody moved. Something had caught his attention and gave him the idea of a picture he could use to show the relationship between himself, the Father and them. It could have been the tendrils of a vine, or a cluster of grapes framed in the window space. Or, perhaps, as he stood it was possible for him to see the moonlight reflecting on the richly decorated gates of the temple, carved with an enormous vine and embellished with gold and jewels.

There are some fanciful interpretations of the opening verses of this chapter. Yet the allegory is clear enough; there are five points to notice.

Jesus is the authentic vine

The 'vine' was frequently used in the Old Testament as a symbol of God's people and it often depicts their failure and inability to live up to all that God expected of them. For example: 'Israel was a spreading vine' which had 'brought forth fruit for' itself (Hosea 10:1). This is remarkable because the vine normally brings forth fruit that is used by others to make their wine. As a nation they were expected to produce the choicest crop, but they 'yielded only bad fruit' (Isaiah 5:2). In contrast Jesus was 'the true (authentic) vine' (verse 1). His richly fruitful life and death was solely in the service of others. Where Israel failed, Jesus succeeded. This is the last time Jesus will use the pronoun and the verb together (literally: 'I–I am'); so it has the force of 'I– I really am the authentic vine'.

The Father is the vinedresser

'My Father is the gardener' (verse 1). The word means 'farmer' and describes someone who worked the land and tilled the soil. Although 'gardener' isn't an incorrect translation, it doesn't quite express the hard work and devotion involved. The text is speaking of a man who wasn't in any sense an amateur; this is his full-time job. As the work involved the vines it wouldn't be wrong to call him a 'vinedresser'. We see the Father's commitment to produce a harvest from the human race that he had planted and nurtured on this fertile planet (Isaiah 5:1–2).

The disciples are the branches

'I am the vine; you are the branches' (verse 5). Jesus told his disciples that the only possible way for them to survive would be to be vitally, organically and personally linked to him; just as branches are joined to a tree. 'Branch', however, suggests something more mature than is being spoken about here. A better word would be 'tendril', the slender outgrowing of the vine that still had to acquire substance. At the point where the tendril is united with the main stock, it is difficult to be certain whether it is joining the vine, or the vine is joined to it. Both are true; there is reciprocity. We are to 'remain in' him, and he 'remain in' us (verse 4). Eleven times in this chapter Jesus uses the phrase 'remain in me'; emphasizing that there is no possibility of bearing fruit unless 'we remain in the vine'. Apart from him we are helpless (verse 5).

The fruit of the vine

What is the 'fruit' (verse 2) that Jesus is talking about here? Some commentators take it to be evangelism and winning others. While it is true that 'the fields . . . ripe for harvest' (John 4:35) is a picture of those who are ready to be gathered into the kingdom, this passage cannot be speaking about that, because it goes on, 'he cuts off every branch . . . that bears no fruit'. Most of us are shy and reluctant to share our faith, but nowhere in the Bible is it suggested that we might lose our life in Christ if we don't evangelize.

So what is the 'fruit'? It must be the opposite of the 'bad fruit' in Isaiah's song of the vineyard (Isaiah 5:1–30). The rottenness that Alec Motyer literally translates as 'stink-fruit' (verse 2; *The Prophecy of Isaiah*, IVP, 1993, p. 68); fruit that is decaying and mouldering in a way that is plain for all to see. It includes:

- Moral depravity (Isaiah 5:18);

- Spiritual blindness (5:20);

- Intellectual arrogance (5:21);

- Political corruption (5:22).

To use a little-used word, the fruit these branches are expected to bear is 'holiness'. This means that there must be evidence of God in our lives. We must be marked off as belonging to God, in our time and in our culture.

The pruning and cleaning experienced by the branches

The vine is encouraged to be fruitful by vigorous pruning (verse 2) and cleaning (verse 3). The same word is used in both verses. This is done to produce 'fruit' (verse 2), more fruit (verse 2) and 'much fruit' (verse 5). John Stott helpfully points out, 'Jesus does not explain specifically what this pruning is. But we need not doubt that pain, sorrow, sickness, suffering, loss, bereavement, disappointment and frustrated ambition are all part of the pruning activity of God the gardener' (*Christ the Liberator*, Hodder & Stoughton, 1972, p. 52). To the non-gardener pruning can often appear to have gone too far; sometimes there seems to be nothing left. But the real gardener knows what he is doing and the following year the blooms and the growth are better than ever. We can be certain that the 'Father . . . gardener' knows what he is doing, and when we feel his pruning-knife it is because he wants to see fruit in our lives. The consequences of bearing fruit are threefold:

- Prayer will be answered (verse 7);
- The Father will be glorified (verse 8);
- We will experience joy (verse 11).

Questions

1. How does a knowledge of the Old Testament background of the vine imagery help us to understand what Jesus is saying here?
2. In practical terms, how can we 'remain in' Jesus? What sort of

things weaken or strengthen our bond with him?

3. What in our lives is the equivalent of the 'fruit' that the vine bears? How fruitful would you say you are? How do you know?

4. Have you experienced anything which could be described as 'pruning' recently? Why has it happened? Share in your group and support those who are not yet able to learn from their experiences.

John 15:9–17

The consequences of being a disciple – 1

There are pluses and minuses involved in being a disciple. On the positive side there is joy and knowledge that the Father wants us to have fulfilment.

The multiplication of blessing

We see the hand of Jesus at work in the lives of true disciples; they are chosen and appointed (verse 16) by him and it is helpful to list actually what we have been chosen for.

Love: a stranger to this planet

Notice all the things that are said about love (verses 9–10, 12–13 and 17). In his first letter John says 'how great is the love that the Father has lavished on us' (1 John 3:1). Originally the word 'great' was used to describe a 'foreign visitor'. That fits in well with what we are told here. The love that we are to remain in and show each other (verse 12) is exactly the same love that the

Father had for Jesus, and that Jesus has for us (verse 9). Just how alien this is to our normal way of living can be seen in its willingness to sacrifice and 'lay down . . . life' (verse 13). The NIV follows the more forceful manuscripts at verse 17 and leaves out 'that' in the middle of the verse. So the correct reading is: 'This is my command: Love each other.'

Joy: the serious business of heaven

The result of obeying the command is 'joy' (verse 11). It is remarkable how often joy is used to summarize all that happens to a Christian. C. S. Lewis called his autobiography *Surprised by Joy*; in it he tells the story of his life as it moved from complete disbelief to the place where he found the reality of Christ. C. S. Lewis called joy 'the serious business of heaven'. In the sixteenth century, when the Bible was first translated into English, William Tyndale described Christianity as 'good, merry, glad and joyfull tydings, that maketh a mannes hert glad, and maketh hym singe, dance and leepe for joy'. Obedience brings deep joy.

On being a friend of Jesus

Most people have a small circle of friends and a wider circle of acquaintances. The word 'friend' (verse 14) here means 'a friend at court' and describes the inner circle surrounding a king. We have already noticed that in Bible times the 'best man' was known as 'the bridegroom's friend' (p. 63). Throughout the Bible we read of those who regarded it a privilege to be known as servants of God (Deuteronomy 34:5). But Jesus is telling his disciples that he has something better for them, 'I have called you friends.' In the New Testament there is no tension between being a 'servant' and a 'friend' because Jesus is the 'Servant King'. T. W. Manson said, 'in the kingdom of God, service is not a stepping-stone to nobility; it is nobility, the only kind of nobility that is recognized.'

Chosen to be partners

In our world today it would be regarded as politically incorrect to suggest that anyone was a servant, whereas it was regarded as an honour by men and women of the Bible. The original word would be even less acceptable; it was 'slave' and in the ancient world slaves were no more than living tools who knew nothing of their master's business (verse 15). So the appointment as 'friends' includes an elevation to a new intimacy with Jesus and a partnership 'to go and bear fruit – fruit that will last' (verse 16).

Shop windows of blessing

Fruit that will stand the test of time will be tangible, cogent evidence that Christianity actually works. Evidence that we really are 'branches' (verse 5), 'disciples' (verse 8) and his 'friends' (verse 14) will be 'fruit' (verse 16) and real fruit always has within it seeds for yet more fruit still.

Joining the family circle

There is a supernatural progression through these verses. We begin as bare 'branches' and end as those that can bear 'fruit'. The consequence of being influenced by Jesus enough to produce fruit means that we are in touch with him enough to know the Father's will. The result: 'ask whatever you wish, and it will be given you' (verse 7); and 'the Father will give you whatever you ask in my name' (verse 16).

Prayer is not getting our will done in heaven; it is getting the Father's will done on earth. All that happens to the 'branches' (disciples) prepares them for this.

Questions

1. If real love does not come naturally to us, how can we obey the command to love each other? Does it mean that we have to feel loving? How can this be?

2. What does it mean in practice to be a 'friend of Jesus'?
3. What exactly is 'joy'? Can unbelievers experience it? Why/
   why not? How would you help those who have no joy,
   Christians and others?

John 15:18 – 16:4

The consequences of being a disciple – 2

**We have looked at the blessings that inevitably come
to disciples; now we must look at the other side of
the coin, and note the down-side of discipleship,
hatred and persecution.**

The world's hatred

When John says, 'If the world hates you . . .'
(verse 18) he is not doubting that this will be
the disciple's experience. The 'if' here means 'since'. So, as
disciples called to love we mustn't be under any misapprehension about how the world will respond to us; it will 'hate' us.
William Temple says that the world 'would not hate angels for
being angelic; but it does hate men for being Christians. It
grudges them their new character; it is tormented by their peace;
it is infuriated by their joy' (*Readings in St John's Gospel*,
Macmillan, 1945, p. 272). Jesus puts his finger on the reason for
the world's hatred; it is because we 'do not belong to the world'
(verse 19). There is a sense in which we do belong to the world;
we were born into it and have grown up in it but our redemption
means that Christ has chosen us out of the world. You can
immediately see what Jesus means if you note that the 'world'

here means this 'sinful world system'. The world hates us because we are not part of its system. It will always oppose those who don't conform.

Responsibility and blessing in a dark hour

'If I had not come and spoken to them, they would not be guilty of sin' (verse 22). The fact that knowledge of Christ and the experience of his blessing bring with them a responsibility is never far from John's mind. Jesus puts it another way: 'If I had not done among them what no-one else did, they would not be guilty of sin' (verse 24). Throughout this gospel it is made quite plain that the Jews were not guiltless in their rejection of Jesus. Had Jesus not visited this planet, they might have had an excuse. But they don't; neither do we for that matter.

The Holy Spirit

We will consider what John has to say at this point about the Holy Spirit when we get to the next chapter, where he deals more fully with the Holy Spirit's work (16:5–15).

The inevitability of persecution

Seven times in this final talk with the disciples Jesus uses the expression, 'All this I have told you'; we are not sure why, but John seems to like having a neat pattern of sevens. For example, in the public ministry of Jesus there are seven sermons and seven miracles (John 2–12). The phrase Jesus uses is in the perfect tense which gives a sense of solemnity to all he has said in the upper room. Jesus says he has told them these things so that they won't go astray. The word 'astray' described the stick that is the trigger for a trap which could be pulled away, trapping birds in a net; so a better translation would be 'so you won't be trapped into going astray' (verse 1). Notice in verses 2–4:

▶ The form this persecution will take:
　'They will put you out of the synagogue.'

▶ Its severity:

'A time is coming when anyone who kills you will think he offering a service to God.'

▶ Who will do this:

It will be the people from the synagogues.

▶ The reason for it:

'They will do such things because they have not known the Father or me.'

▶ A warning:

'I did not tell you this at first because I was with you.'

Questions

1. Why do people in the world around us respond so negatively to the followers of Jesus? Face the reasons honestly, good and bad.
2. What pressure do you come under for your Christian faith? In what ways might this lead to your going 'astray'? How does what Jesus says here help?
3. How should the church prepare itself for persecution and how should we respond to it when it comes?

John 16:5–15

Focus on the Holy Spirit

Jesus gives us a concentrated and detailed consideration of the work of the Holy Spirit.

The helper at work

Jesus uses the word 'Counsellor' for the fourth time in 16:7. We have already noticed (p. 157) that 'Strengthener' would be a better word, because Jesus is talking about someone called alongside to help. We will list the things that are true of this helper.

He is the Spirit of truth

Jesus has already spoken about this (14:6) and will do so again (16:13). All that Jesus said and did was linked to the truth (3:21); he called himself 'the truth' (14:6). He is absolute truth, there are no half-measures with him. We often find it easier to deal with half-truths because the whole truth can be very uncomfortable. But the Spirit who lives in us is 'the Spirit of truth' and we will 'grieve' him (Ephesians 4:30) if we don't make truth our aim. If you want to know what it means to 'grieve' the Holy Spirit, look at the story of the rich young ruler where the same word is translated 'sad' (Mark 10:22).

He is sent from the Father

Jesus declares that he will 'send' the Holy Spirit 'from the Father' (15:26). We probably don't think of this as radical and something that would cause great division in the church. But the statement in the Nicene creed (AD 325) about the Spirit 'proceeding from the Father' comes from this verse. The whole question of the relationship of the Spirit and the other members of the godhead caused the split between the Eastern and Western church (the Roman Catholic and the Greek Orthodox) in the fourth century. In the Nicene creed we say that we believe that the Holy Spirit proceeds from the Father and the Son.

He testifies about Jesus

The idea of 'testifying' is very important in John's gospel and the work of the Spirit is spoken of as testifying about Jesus. The Father 'testifies' (5:32), and so does Jesus on his own behalf (8:14). The things that Jesus did bear testimony to him (5:36), as does the Bible (5:39). John now adds to this by saying it is the work of the Spirit to testify about Jesus (15:26) and in the next verse says we too are to 'testify' (15:27). At the very least this means when we are witnessing we will not be doing it alone.

The departure of Jesus brings the advantage of the Spirit

The departure of Jesus will cause the disciples grief (verse 6), but it will also bring the Holy Spirit. 'Unless I go away . . . (he) will not come to you' (verse 7). The word 'grief' means 'deep sadness tinged with regret'; it is used four times in this chapter and nowhere else in the gospel.

The Spirit will bring a conviction about sin

The word 'convict' (verse 8) is not easy to translate but it tells us how the Spirit works in an unbeliever's life. It can mean to convince, expose, reveal, show, teach and even cross-examine. The Spirit will do whatever is necessary to make the unbeliever aware of the guilt of sin, whereas the plain words of Jesus alone can't do this, 'because men do not believe in (him)' (verse 9).

The righteousness that results from the cross

At first it is not obvious what is meant here (verses 8, 10). When the Spirit convicts the world of sin it means that the world will discover just how sinful it is. But when the world is convicted about righteousness it doesn't mean that it will see how righteous it is; quite the reverse. The righteousness referred to here is the righteousness that comes to us through the death of Jesus. It is a work of the Holy Spirit to reveal this.

Conviction about judgment

Again, this is difficult to understand (verses 8, 11). The world is under God's judgment, but this can't be what the Spirit is teaching here, because Jesus' statement goes on, 'the prince of this world now stands condemned'. The 'prince of this world' (12:31) is the evil one. And the point that Jesus is making is that the cross wasn't merely a little encounter with the devil, it was a decisive victory with eternal consequences. It is the work of the Spirit to reveal that the devil now stands condemned. This is the judgment Jesus is talking about.

The Spirit, the Guide and the Glory

The disciples (including us today) will never reach the stage of knowing everything about spiritual truth. It is the function of the Spirit to guide disciples into all truth (verse 13). This means we must seek his guidance, particularly when we read the Bible. The Spirit will glorify Jesus by taking what is his and making it known to us (verse 14).

Questions

1. What practical implications are there in the fact that the Holy Spirit is the Spirit of 'truth'?
2. What does Jesus say that the Holy Spirit will do? How do these different aspects apply to us today?
3. How far do you see the Holy Spirit at work in the world beyond the church?

John 16:16–33

Focus on the disciples

The pain and confusion involved in Jesus' departure will give way to joy as the Spirit assures the disciples of God's love for them and presence with them.

From sorrow to joy

The focus now moves from the Holy Spirit to the disciples. In the twentieth century we live lives of comparative ease. By contrast New Testament times were harsh, and for the ordinary person largely miserable. There was no unemployment benefit, no Health Service; there were no pensions, holidays, no time off and opportunities to relax were rare. If you had lived in those times and somehow managed to get hold of a New Testament (forgive the anachronism) you would have been struck by the note of joy and the radiant optimism that began with the coming of Christ and filled its pages and was enjoyed by his followers. Notice:

The disciples' confusion

From our point of view, it is easy to understand what Jesus meant when he said, 'In a little while you will see me no more, and then after a little while you will see me' (verse 16). The early disciples didn't have a New Testament that would tell them about the resurrection, however, so their confusion and apprehension were understandable. When the events of the first Good Friday took place, it must have seemed that evil had won.

The disciples' joy

Jesus spots the bewilderment of the disciples and tries to help. 'I tell you the truth (note the formula!), you will weep and mourn while the world rejoices. You will grieve, but your grief will turn to joy' (verse 20). The 'you' is emphatic; 'you – you of all people – will experience real anguish' while for 'the world', those opposed to God, the crucifixion would mean 'rejoicing' because they would think that Jesus and his disciples were finished.

This is such an important lesson that Jesus repeats it in different words to emphasize that 'no-one will take away (their) joy' (verse 22). Like childbirth, the eventual joy meant that the painful event was soon forgotten. Their time of grief will be real but the dominant note of the section is joy. 'I will see you again and you will rejoice, and no-one will take away your joy' (verse 22).

The disciples' faith

The key to this section is 'The Father . . . loves you because you have loved me and have believed that I came from God' (verse 27). The disciples' love for and belief in Jesus are in a tense that speaks of their permanence. In other words their faith and love for Jesus was a settled conviction. This has enabled Jesus to begin with important teaching on prayer (note the formula), 'I tell you the truth' (verse 23).

The disciples' peace

Finally, Jesus told his disciples, 'I have told you these things, so that . . . you may have peace' (verse 33). We have noticed already (pp. 155–156) that in our European culture we understand 'peace' in a Greek way rather than in the Jewish sense. For the Jew, 'peace' wasn't merely the absence of war and fighting, it was a many-faceted thing, which contained at the very least the idea of victory, health, a time of security and calm and 'the age of the Messiah'. In contemporary language what Jesus is saying to his disciples is 'Cheer up! It is a fact, I have overcome the world. Therefore begin to enjoy all the blessings of the Messianic age.'

Questions

1. Does Jesus' repeated teaching about the 'little while' (verses 16–24) have anything to teach us? What do we wait for?
2. What can we expect to receive if we ask in Jesus' name (verse 24)? Is there any limit? Is it happening?
3. In what sense has Jesus 'overcome the world' (verse 33)? It doesn't look much like it!

Prayer in the name of Christ

Prayer must always be in the name of Jesus; because it is who Jesus is and what he has done that makes prayer such a mighty weapon for believers. And prayer 'in Jesus' name' won't distance disciples from the Father because he himself (verse 27) loves them too. This doesn't mean we are to use 'the name of Jesus' as a formula we tag on the end of every prayer. Praying 'in the name of Jesus' will affect the content of the prayers too. The disciples' prayer will not be deliberately outside the will of Christ. It will be prayer in accordance with all his name implies. It is prayer that proceeds from a faith in Christ and continues to be constrained by that faith.

Jesus prays for himself

This chapter contains what is called Jesus' 'high-priestly prayer' in which he prays for himself, his disciples and the church through the centuries to come.

 It was Clement of Alexandria (*c.* AD 150–215) who said that in this prayer Jesus was a high priest acting on behalf of his people. It is a good description. We should note the following:

The physical posture of Jesus while at prayer

'He looked towards heaven and prayed' (verse 1). Most people adopt a special posture when they pray; today we bow our heads and shut our eyes. Jesus did as the people of his time would do; he raised his head instead of bowing it, and kept his eyes open instead of closing them.

He spoke to Father

'Father' (verse 1). We're so used to addressing God like this that we forget how unusual it was in Bible times to use the language of the family in prayer. Six times Jesus addressed God as 'Father' (verses 1, 5, 11, 21, 24, 25).

The right moment had arrived

Several times we have noticed that Jesus felt that his time had not come. But now it had (verse 1), so the significant moment of his ministry had arrived. His death and resurrection were at hand.

It is the moment for him to be glorified

To 'glorify' normally speaks of adding 'weight and splendour' to make a person more majestic, but we've noticed that in John's vocabulary it is often used to refer to the cross of Jesus. Here the word is really used in both senses; Jesus is saying, 'Father, the moment for the cross has come, help me to magnify you.'

Amazing giving

The idea of 'giving' comes seventeen times in this prayer; thirteen times it speaks of the Father giving to the Son and four times of the Son's gifts to his disciples. For John the Father is someone who gives and gives and gives. He 'gave his one and only Son' and he continues to give. John used the idea of giving in much the same way that Paul spoke of grace.

The emphasis here

The emphasis here is on the Father having given (granted) the son 'authority over all people that he might give eternal life to all those you have given him' (verse 2). This is followed with a definition of 'eternal life' (verse 3). Jesus doesn't say that knowing the Father and the Son will bestow life, but is life; that is, a new quality of life.

Jesus speaks about himself in an unusual way

The prayer began smoothly enough with Jesus referring to himself as the 'Son' (verse 1). We would expect him to move on to use the pronoun 'I', but instead he speaks of himself as 'Jesus Christ' (verse 3). Probably an explanation is inserted here, so that there can be no misunderstanding about the nature of his ministry. He was 'sent' by 'the only true God'.

A glimpse of pre-history and a glance at post-history

Through the lowliness and humility of his life, Jesus has brought the Father 'glory on earth' (verse 4). Now he looks ahead to the restoration of the 'glory' (in the sense of brilliance, honour and majesty) that he had with the Father 'before the world began' (verse 5).

Questions

---

1. To what extent is your view of God shaped by the assertion that he is an amazing Giver? What has he given you?
2. How does what Jesus says here help to explain what eternal life is all about?
3. What does 'glory' mean? How does our imitation of Christ bring glory to the Father?

John 17:6–19

Jesus prays for his disciples

Knowing far more clearly than they do what is in store for them, Jesus earnestly prays for his disciples.

Jesus turns from praying for himself to focus on the needs of his small band of followers. At the moment they were unaware that they were about to face the biggest crisis of their lives. The 'going away' that Jesus had spoken about would involve his arrest, trial and crucifixion before he returned to heaven. One disciple had already betrayed him, one will deny him three times and all, in one way or another, will desert him. So Jesus prays for them.

Disciples should be recognized by four important characteristics:

Disciples must focus on the truth (verses 11–13)

Jesus prays that the Father will protect them 'by the power of his name' (verse 11). 'God's name' is a summary of all that he is, and all that he has revealed about himself. The result will be that the disciples will be united as the Father and the Son are one. The disciples' pathway to unity will be commitment to truth.

They must reflect holiness (verses 14–17)

The truth that keeps the disciples will be seen in their lives by the way they are kept 'from the evil one' (verse 15) and are sanctified (verse 17) or 'made holy'. There are few things more important for us than to rediscover true biblical holiness. Holiness is the stamp on our lives that we belong to God. God's people have always swung to one of two extremes in trying to achieve holiness. Either we have given up the struggle and conformed to the world (that is our problem today) or we withdraw as the Pharisees did. The 'world' is referred to fifteen times in this chapter; so it is obviously important. The disciples were 'up to their eyes' in the world, but somehow they were not part of it. We must be like that too.

There must be total commitment to mission (verses 18–19)

Jesus says, 'As you sent me into the world, I have sent them'. The best way to send an idea is to wrap it up in a person; that is what the Father did when he sent the Son from heaven. And that is what the Son does (and is still doing) with his disciples.

There must be a concentration on unity (verses 20–26)

Technically this is part of the next section of the prayer, but as Jesus has already prayed for his disciples' unity we will look at it here. He now prays 'that all of them may be one' verse 21), brought to a complete unity (verse 23). Lack of unity among

God's people doesn't make sense. One of the great Puritan writers summed it up, 'For wolves to worry the lambs is no wonder, but for one lamb to worry another, is unnatural and monstrous' (Thomas Brookes, in I.D.E. Thomas, *Puritan Quotations*, Moody Press, p. 304). God's people should be like an orchestra, having taken their note from one instrument, they are now perfectly in tune with each other. We take our standard of unity from Jesus (the unity he has with the Father) and that means we should be in perfect harmony with all other disciples.

Questions

1. How does the suggestion that the way to reach unity is 'commitment to truth' work out in practice for you in your situation?
2. What does it mean to be 'holy'? How do we get there?
3. What are you doing to communicate the Christian ideas that have been 'wrapped up' in you?
4. Are there two worlds, spiritual and material, or are these two ways of looking at one truth?

What is a disciple?

A disciple is someone who follows a teacher in order to learn a subject or trade. The word literally means 'learner'; the best English equivalent is 'apprentice'. 'Student' isn't the right word, because that suggests academic theory and discipleship is about practical teaching. A disciple would often live with his master and would endeavour to put into practice all that he had learnt.

A description of discipleship

There are three things we need to note:

- *The disciples belonged to Jesus.* Three times Jesus says the Father has 'given' the disciples to him (verses 6, 9). So the disciples who had once been part of the world now belong to Jesus.

- *They knew the Father.* The Father had given them to the Son who had 'revealed' the Father to them, and had given them 'the words' that had been given him.

- *They lived in the world.* Jesus was not going to be in the world much longer but the disciples would be (verse 11). Although they had been given to Jesus 'out of the world' they would still remain in it. Like Jesus they had to live in the world but not be part of it (verse 14).

Although a disciple was one of the original group of men who followed Jesus, we need to note what is being said, because if we are trying to follow Jesus these things must be reflected in our lives too.

What Jesus prayed for his disciples

The main thrust of the prayer is that the Father will 'protect' them from any evil influence that would stop them reflecting their essential identity to the world in which they live (verses 11, 15).

Jesus prays for us

**In praying for those who will believe in him,
through the witness of the first disciples,
Jesus prays for all of us first.**

The emphasis is now on future believers: 'I pray also for those who will believe in me through their message' (verse 20). It is worth noting that a change is taking place. Jesus moves from talking about 'them' (that is the original band of 'disciples') and he starts to refer to 'those' who will believe. As he looks ahead to the church, he mentions three things.

The unity of the future church

We have already begun to look at this, but we will look at it again in context here because the ecumenism of our generation sometimes gets hold of the wrong end of the stick.

What is this unity like?

It is like the unity of the original group of disciples and the unity of the Father and Son (verse 21). You can't get any closer than that.

How can this unity be achieved?

The answer is found in the truth that God has revealed. Through this prayer there has been an emphasis on revealed truth. Unity is found in the 'name' (verse 11), the 'message' (verse 20), and 'glory' (verse 22); these are all the same thing, part of the revealed character of God.

Why is unity so important?

Unity is important 'so that the world may believe that you have sent me' (verse 21) and also to demonstrate the Father's love (verse 23). So the object and the purpose of unity is stated clearly. As Thomas Manton put it, 'Divisions in the church breed atheism in the world' (*An Exposition of John 17*, Marchallton, 1958).

When will this true unity be achieved?

'Father, I want those you have given me to be with me where I am, and to see my glory, the glory you have given me because you loved me before the creation of the world' (verse 24). The final unity of seeing Father, Son and church reflecting the glory of heaven will only be enjoyed in eternity when God permanently establishes his kingdom for ever. This doesn't meant that we need to leave working for unity until we get to heaven, but it does mean that we shouldn't accept a spurious uniformity in place of the real thing.

Looking forward to the glory of Jesus (verse 24)

Future believers are now referred to as 'those you have given me' and we are now told that one day they will see the glory that the Father has given to Jesus. As we have noticed, John often uses the word 'glory' to speak of lowly service, but this time the word is used in its accepted sense of splendour and majesty.

Looking back in love (verses 25–26)

This high-priestly prayer is brought to a conclusion not with a request, but with a lingering look back over the time the disciples have been with him. Jesus calls the Father, 'Righteous Father', a form of address that is only found here in the New Testament. Jesus says he has made this Father 'known to' the disciples and that he will continue to do so. We can presume that this will be done through the future work of the Holy Spirit. Then this extraordinary prayer is brought to an end with the unusual thought that it is only as Jesus abides in his people that they will know the love of God. There is no way that this love can be separated from the presence of Christ.

Questions

1. List ways in which this section helps us in personal discipleship.
2. In what way can modern efforts towards church unity 'sometimes get hold of the wrong end of the stick'? How then can true unity be brought about?
3. Do 'divisions in the church breed atheism in the world'? Find examples. What part does the press play in exaggerating the church's problems? Pray for all journalists.

THE TRIAL, DEATH AND RESURRECTION OF JESUS

John 18:1 – 20:31

John 18:1–11

Jesus is arrested

At this point in the narrative Jesus ceases to dominate events by his actions and submits to the demands of his enemies. But he is still in charge.

 At the beginning of chapter eighteen, John takes up the account recorded by the other gospel writers, but he gives us his own perspective on these events. His emphasis is that Jesus is in charge of everything that happens and master of every situation.

The arrest in the olive grove

While Matthew and Mark inform us that it was called 'Gethsemane' (meaning 'oil-press', Matthew 26:36; Mark 14:32) John adds that it was a garden (verse 1). The translators combine these two pieces of information and presume that the garden was an 'olive grove'. It was on the far side of the Kidron Valley; the word translated 'valley' means a winter torrent, so presumably it was perfectly dry in the summer, but in the winter became a raging, over-flowing torrent. Space was too expensive and limited in Jerusalem for gardens, but many rich people had them outside the city. Jesus and his disciples often retreated to this particular spot

187

(verse 2). Surprisingly, John doesn't say anything about the agony that Jesus experienced in the garden, although he does record that Jesus spoke about the 'cup' of suffering he must drink.

Judas is often referred to as 'Judas, who betrayed him' (e.g. verse 2). It is interesting that the writers of the New Testament don't go out of their way to blame him, or to blacken his character in the way a writer of fiction might. The gospel writers just state the facts.

The party accompanying Judas included 'officials from the chief priests and Pharisees' and 'a detachment of soldiers'. This is a technical term describing a tenth part of a legion (a legion was 6,000 soldiers, so a detachment was 600 armed men). But the term doesn't have to be taken literally, any more than we would expect to be, if we spoke about a company of soldiers. John is simply saying that there were enough soldiers to make the arrest.

Note that the master of the situation knew 'all that was going to happen to him' (verse 4). Jesus wasn't taken by surprise. The soldiers identify him by name and the place he comes from. Three times Jesus uses the solemn and emphatic 'I–I am' in answer.

Some surprising reactions

At the times of the great festivals (13:1) it must have been a daily occurrence for a squad of soldiers to be sent out to deal with a zealot or a protest somewhere in the city. The Roman military were not squeamish, especially when sent to arrest a single Jewish peasant from somewhere in the country. However, there was something different about this man. He stood his ground and he looked them straight in the eye as he answered their questions. Such was their surprise, that 'they drew back and fell to the ground' (verse 6).

The disciples were unwilling to let their master be arrested without a protest. Peter drew his 'sword' (verse 10). The word probably means a 'long knife', another word is used for the sword you would fight with (Luke 2:35). Whatever the weapon, there was no doubt about Peter's intention or what he did. He cut off the ear of Malchus. Jesus forbade further action or resistance and told Peter to put away his sword. The negative way that Jesus said, 'Shall I not drink . . .?' leaves us in no doubt that he was determined to go through the difficulties that lay ahead.

Questions

1. Why do you think that John does not mention the agonized prayer of Jesus in Gethsemane? (Read Matthew 26:36–46.)
2. It has been said that Jesus' command of the situation ceased to be active at this point (making things happen) but passive (allowing things to happen to him). How does the narrative suggest this? Does it help us to understand what Jesus was doing?
3. What *was* Peter trying to do with his sword? Is there any place for violence in the Christian life? Why?/why not?

John 18:12–27

Peter's nerve fails

Jesus is accused before Annas, the former high priest who still dominated the Jewish religious scene, and then before Caiaphas the current high priest. At this point Peter denies that he knows Jesus.

None of the gospel writers give us a complete picture of the trials of Jesus; therefore we are left with some uncertainties. One uncertainty that we have is because we have little information about Jewish criminal procedure; we don't know why Jesus was taken before Annas.

Peter's first denial (verses 15–18)

It is easy to begin to picture this scene because we have already looked at some of the words: the 'courtyard' was the 'sheep pen' (10:1; see p. 120) and the 'door' the 'gate' (10:1). So what is being described is a building around an open courtyard. At one point there is an opening giving access to the central area. In the opening, which may or may not be covered, the servants and officials were standing around a charcoal brazier to keep warm and Peter was standing with them warming himself. A female slave is in charge of the door, and feels sure Peter was one of the arrested man's disciples. 'I am not,' said Peter firmly. It was an unfortunate statement because Peter was now committed to telling lies. One small step in the direction of evil can often lead to others.

The examination before Annas (verses 19–24)

The 'high priest' now questioned Jesus about his disciples and his teaching. This must be a reference to Annas (verse 13) because after the interrogation he would send Jesus to 'Caiaphas the high priest' (verse 24). Caiaphas was the son-in-law of Annas. Presumably Caiaphas was the official high priest, perhaps recently appointed by Pilate (11:49), but many would still regard Annas as the real high priest, because the job and the title were for life.

What is described was highly illegal. Jewish law made it clear that the accused could not be invited to incriminate himself. Guilt must be established by witnesses. That is why Jesus asked, 'Why question me?' This appeal caused an official to strike 'him in the face'. Originally, this was a blow given with something like a piece of wood, but by this time had come to mean a clip with the hand, especially an open hand. The official 'slapped Jesus in the face' is what we are being told. It was as illegal as much of the interrogation.

The second and third denial of Peter (verses 25–27)

We return to the scene with Peter 'warming himself' by the fire. Again he is questioned about his relationship with Jesus. The question is put in a way that expects a negative answer. And Peter gave an unequivocal reply: 'I am not.' A relative of Malchus, whose ear Peter had cut off, challenged him, 'Didn't I see you with him?' Peter again denied it; and the cock started to crow, precisely as Jesus had foreseen (13:38).

Peter's failure is obvious for all to see, but what is often not acknowledged is the fact that we would have not fared much better. In groups there is a reluctance for one person to go in an opposite direction from the rest of the group. In reality, however, it is not as difficult as it seems to remain loyal to Christ, if we firmly and gently state that we are Christians.

Questions

1. How does Peter's experience illustrate the tendency of sin to grow out of control?
2. What was 'highly illegal' about these proceedings?
3. How can Jesus have remained in control of events when he had surrendered himself to the authorities? Is there anything we can learn about the proper exercise of authority such as Jesus showed?

The Roman domination of Judea

The Romans had set up a complex bureaucracy to run Judea. The Emperor Tiberius had appointed Pilate the fifth procurator of Judea in AD 26 and he had complete control of the province. The troops under his command consisted of 1 *ala* (about 120 men) of cavalry and four or five detachments of infantry (about 3,000 men). These soldiers were stationed at Caesarea with a detachment always on garrison duty at Jerusalem in the fortress of Antonia. Pilate, like all Roman governors, had the power of life and death. He could reverse sentences passed by the Sanhedrin which had to be submitted to him for ratification. He also appointed the high priest and was in control of the temple and its funds. Even the vestments of the high priest were kept in his custody and would only be released for use at the major festivals. When the procurator took up residence in Jerusalem he would bring extra soldiers to patrol the city. Everything in Judea was controlled by Pilate although in practice he allowed the Jewish authorities to run the city on a day-to-day basis. This explains why Jesus had both a Jewish and a Roman trial.

John 18:28–40

Jesus before Pilate – 1

The Jews hope that Pilate will ratify the death sentence, but the governor, torn between Roman justice and the fear of unrest, looks for a compromise.

John hasn't really told us anything about the trial before Annas and Caiaphas, apart from the fact that it had taken place. The other writers provide us with some information.
We know that Jesus appeared before the Sanhedrin (the Jewish parliament) and they found him guilty of blasphemy 'worthy of death' (Matthew 26:66; Mark 14:64). The problem was that the Sanhedrin had no authority to carry out such a death penalty.

Before Pilate

Once before Pilate, the Jewish authorities have a problem. They can't accuse Jesus of being guilty of 'blasphemy against Jehovah' because that wouldn't wash with the Romans at all. They have to find an accusation that will carry the death penalty as a Roman offence. It is clear from what follows that Pilate regarded Jesus as completely innocent. Three times he says to the Jews that he can see no basis for charging Jesus (verse 38; 19:4, 6). Pilate was not going to punish Jesus merely because 'the Jews didn't like him. Eventually Pilate saw a way out: 'It is your custom for me to release to you one prisoner at the time of the Passover. Do you want me to release Jesus?' The Jews shout, 'No, not him! Give us Barabbas!'

King of the Jews (verse 33)

Pilate's questions show that there was more to the event than John has recorded. When he asks, 'Are you the king of the Jews?' the *you* is emphatic, 'Are *you* the king of the Jews?' It is possible that Pilate was expecting some sort of revolutionary that the area produced from time to time. But one look at Jesus would have shown him that such an idea was wide of the mark. 'My kingdom is not of this world,' Jesus replied (verse 36). We have noticed that 'kingdom' speaks about 'reign' rather than realm, but there is also a sense of activity behind the statement. It is as though Jesus was saying, 'Yes, I am *sovereign* to those who follow me.'

What kind of death? (verse 32)

To understand what is going on, it is important that we look at the legal and political situation. But John is talking about something much deeper. 'This happened so that the words Jesus had spoken indicating the kind of death he was going to die would be fulfilled.' The Jewish leaders could do all they wished and Pilate could try not to be involved, but it was God's plan that was going to be fulfilled. Jesus was going to die for the sins of the human race (1:29) and it was to be death by crucifixion (12:32–33).

Questions

1. Why did Jesus have to be tried by Pilate as well as the high priest? If Jesus had been stoned to death by a mob serving the priests, would it make any difference to our Christian beliefs?
2. How does John continue to emphasize God's sovereign control of what takes place?
3. If modern states are 'secular' (religion is not their business) how far are they doing what Pilate did?

The Governor's palace

'The Jews led Jesus . . . to the palace of the Roman governor' (verse 28). John uses its proper name, *praetorium*, but the translators think that 'palace' is more understandable in the twentieth century. *Praetorium* was the name for the headquarters of the commanding officer of a Roman military camp, or the headquarters of a Roman governor such as Pilate. While in Judea, Pilate normally lived in the palace Herod the Great had built for himself in Caesarea; but he made it a point always to be in Jerusalem at the time of the major festivals so he could quell any disturbances. While in Jerusalem he lived in the *praetorium*, but we are not sure where this was situated. It was either Herod's palace on the western wall of the city, or the Fortress of Antonia (named after Mark Antony) which was north-west of the temple complex and connected by steps to the temple's outer court.

Barabbas (verse 40)

Barabbas was a murderer arrested for his part in an insurrection (Luke 23:19). The first part of his name 'Bar' means 'son of' and 'abba' was the Aramaic (the local Hebrew dialect) for 'father'. So 'son of a father' was probably equivalent to the English 'son of a gun', the name put into a ship's log on a British 'man-of-war' to record the birth of an illegitimate child. To put it another way, the Jews wanted the 'son of a father' released so that the 'Son of the Father' could die!

John 19:1–16a

Jesus before Pilate – 2

Pilate veers between vicious cruelty and apparent compassion, curiosity and fear. Fear finally triumphs.

The flogging and the sentence

Early in Acts we are told that Pilate had decided to let Jesus go (Acts 3:13); and it certainly appears that he did everything possible to release him. At the end of the last chapter we saw him trying to do this by using the custom of freeing a prisoner at Passover. But the crowd was adamant that they wanted Barabbas, so Pilate had Jesus flogged. He even permitted the soldiers' crude horseplay, probably hoping the crowd would change their mind when they saw a Jew and Jewish things being so savagely mocked. At this point we're told that 'from then on, Pilate tried to set Jesus free' (verse 12). It was no use; the Jews had little or no concern for Pilate's scruples and insisted on Jesus being crucified.

The soldiers' horseplay

It was not every day that a 'king' was to be executed so the soldiers indulged in savage derision. They improvised a crown of thorns and the sort of robe that would befit a king. Because of its cost purple cloth was much prized in the ancient world and was associated with royalty. The dye came from the 'throat' of a tiny shellfish called *Murex* caught off the Phoenician coast. The first convert in Europe was an enterprising Asian business woman who traded in 'purple cloth' (Acts 16:14). The soldiers obviously relished the opportunity to make fun of Jesus: 'Hail, king of the Jews!' We must not miss the fact that they 'went up to him again *and again*' (verse 3) to do this. There is a sick horror in the sheer persistent repetition of their taunting.

'Here is the man!' (verse 5)

There are many different things hidden in this phrase. In classical Greek it could imply that the man was a *poor* creature. Therefore it could be an expression of Pilate's contempt and his dismissal of the charges against Jesus: 'Look at him! Could *he* ever be confused with a revolutionary?' John could be saying it ironically: 'Here is *the* man; here is perfect manhood. In spite of the mockery, surely you can see that?' But nothing can change the attitude of the Jews; they still look at him and cry 'Crucify! Crucify!' (verse 6).

It is very difficult to understand Pilate. He knew that what the Jewish leaders were saying about Jesus wasn't true and he seems to have regarded him as being innocent. He was obviously an able civil servant who was used to taking decisions. As a province, Palestine bristled with problems and anyone appointed would be expected to govern with a firm, strong and wise hand. Pilate's career seems to have ended in failure. Just after Jesus was crucified there was a revolt in Samaria. It was not regarded as desperately serious, but Pilate put it down with sadistic ferocity and a great list of executions. The Samaritans were always known to be loyal to Rome. The legate of Syria was called in to mediate and eventually Caesar Tiberius called Pilate back to Rome. While Pilate was travelling, Tiberius died. It is not known if Pilate had to face the next emperor, but from that moment Pilate vanishes from history. The lesson that even lesser mortals must learn from Pilate is that if we know the truth, we must state it and do it.

Questions

1. Either: individually spend time 'thinking yourself into' the situation described here. What did Pilate, the 'Jews' and Jesus feel like? Or: divide your group between supporters of Pilate and the Jews and argue your respective cases. What do we learn from this exercise?

2. Jesus 'claimed to be the Son of God' (verse 7). Some people claim that he was only a very good man. Why is it important for us to know what we believe about this question?

3. Can governments ever hope to ignore religion? Share what you know about the church and state in modern times, especially in Russia, China, Eastern Europe, USA.

Flogging

There were three different forms of 'flogging' that could be imposed under Roman law.

- *fustigatio*: A beating given for relatively light offences such as hooliganism, this would be accompanied with severe warnings.

- *flagellatio*: A brutal thrashing imposed on criminals whose offences were more serious.

- *verberatio*: A flogging, the most terrible form of scourging often associated with other punishments like crucifixion.

The prisoner to be flogged would be stripped and tied to a post so that his back was exposed. The instrument was a leather whip of several thongs, each thong fitted with pieces of lead and sharpened bone at various places along its length. In a province such as Judea, the punishment would be given by a soldier and the prisoner would be flogged until the soldier was exhausted or his officer called a halt.

It is remarkable that in an age which was much more violent than our own, the writers don't dwell on the agony of Christ's suffering. In a straightforward way they state the facts and make no attempt to play on the emotions of the readers.

The judge's seat on the Stone Pavement

The place was known as *the Stone Pavement*, or 'Gabbatha', which is an Aramaic word meaning 'the hill of the house'. The area described a piece of tesselated pavement of marble mosaic, on which Pilate's 'judge's seat' (verse 13) was put when as the representative of Rome he made his judicial decisions. Such an area covering about 2,300 square yards has been excavated in the Tower of Antonia. *Judge's seat* is literally 'the step' and means a seat with steps leading up to it; a seat of authority. It is an important New Testament word because it is regularly used for the judgment seat of God (cf. Romans 14:10).

The crucifixion

Jesus' crucifixion is described in simple, factual, unsentimental language.

The routine for crucifixion was always much the same. Once the criminal had been sentenced he would be placed in the centre of a *quaternion* (a squad of four soldiers), the cross would be put on his shoulders and he would carry it to the place of execution. 'Each criminal as part of his punishment carries his own cross on his back' (Plutarch, *The Divine Vengeance*). The prisoner would have to be goaded along the road, as he staggered to the place of crucifixion. Before the group of soldiers an officer would carry a sign bearing the prisoner's crime and offence.

The soldiers and their prisoner are heading for 'the place of the Skull' (verse 17). 'Golgotha' is a transliteration (English letters for Greek) of a Greek word which was already a transliteration of the Aramaic 'Gulgolta' meaning skull. 'Calvary' is from the Latin *calvaria* also meaning skull.

Pilate had written a sign to be fastened to the cross (verse 19). In the three great languages of the ancient world it said, 'JESUS OF NAZARETH, THE KING OF THE JEWS'. In these final chapters John emphasizes the kingship of Jesus. The Jews might have rejected him, the Roman authorities were too spineless to defend him, but John wants everybody to see that he was King. It helped that the inscription was in these three languages. The 'Hebrew' was Aramaic which was the local dialect; Latin was the official language of the government; and Greek was the commonly understood language of the empire. Whoever saw the sign would have been able to read it in one language or another.

One of the perks for the escorting squad of soldiers was the prisoner's clothes. A Jewish man would have five pieces of clothing. His shoes, a belt, a tunic (NIV 'undergarment'), a robe and a turban. The four soldiers have the problem of deciding who would get the fifth piece, the seamless tunic (verse 23). They don't want to tear it so they gamble for it, fulfilling a prophecy from the Old Testament (Psalm 22:18). The seamless robe was unusual. One Jewish historian tells us that the high priest wore such a garment. The slit for the neck was not across the shoulders, but from the middle of the chest to the middle of the back, an unusual design.

The usual crowd had gathered to watch the execution, including a handful of women who knew Jesus. It is not certain if there were three or four women in this group. It hinges on the phrase 'his mother's sister, Mary the wife of Clopas' (verse 25). If this was describing the same person, the group consisted of three women. However it is unlikely that Jesus' mother (unnamed in this gospel) would have had a sister, also called Mary. So it is probably right to suggest that the group consisted of four women. In spite of the agony of the cross Jesus managed to talk to his mother and at least one of the other women.

Jesus died with a cry of victory on his lips. All that he had come to do had been accomplished. John doesn't say anything about the way Jesus said, 'It is finished' (verse 30), but the other writers tell us that it was with a loud cry (Matthew 27:50; Mark 15:27; Luke 23:46). The cry could mean several things. It could simply be saying, 'My life is over', but it is much more likely that, with a shout of triumph, he was saying, 'I've done what the Father sent me to do.'

Questions

1. What is remarkable about the way the sufferings of Jesus are

described here? Why is this? Is it healthy for us to try to imagine the agony of Jesus? Why?/why not?

2. Once again, John emphasizes the kingship of Jesus. How? What does it imply for us?

3. Is the death penalty ever appropriate? If so how can we defend it? If it had not been used in Jesus' time how could we have been saved?

Crucifixion

Crucifixion was the most terrible form of execution. It was originally devised by the Persians. They may have developed it because they regarded the earth as sacred and wanted to avoid defiling the ground with the body of a criminal. It was taken over by the Carthaginians of North Africa and finally commandeered by the Romans. The Romans used it only in the provinces and then largely for slaves; it was never used on mainland Italy and it was unthinkable that a Roman would ever be crucified.

After the victim had been flogged, which was done as much to weaken as to punish, he would carry the horizontal bar of the cross (*patibulum*) to the place of execution. The vertical beam of the gibbet would normally have been fixed in the ground already. The prisoner would then be made to lie on the ground so that his hands could be tied or nailed to the *patibulum*. This cross-bar was then hoisted on to the vertical beam and the victim's feet tied or nailed to the beam. Sometimes there was a 'seat' (*seducula*) which helped support the victim's body, but this actually increased the agony for the sufferer rather than easing it. A lot of our mental images of crucifixion have come down to us from great art, where, to balance the picture, the artist has often painted a tall cross. But wood was a costly commodity and the victims were rarely high in air. Providing their feet were off the ground the execution was effective and equally horrific.

Hyssop

Jesus was thirsty so a sponge soaked in cheap wine (that is what is meant by the word 'vinegar') was given to him on the end of a stalk of hyssop (verse 29). There is a problem here because hyssop is a small bushy plant without a strong central stalk. But the problem is largely resolved when we get the scene into perspective and do not imagine the crucified Jesus high above the soldiers.

Piercing the side of Jesus

John is the only one to give us this detail and it has the ring of an eye-witness about it. Those crucified by the Romans would normally be left until they died and then the scavengers would come and devour the rotting flesh. Under Jewish law, anyone hanged on a gibbet was not to be left overnight (Deuteronomy 21:22–23). If death had to be hurried for any reason (verse 31), the prisoner's legs would be broken (this was called *crucifragium*). Aside from the shock which could kill by itself, it prevented the prisoner pushing upwards and continuing to breathe. What is surprising in these verses is that the legs of Jesus weren't broken, as was the case with the other two, but his side was pierced, which was not part of normal procedure. It isn't clear what the 'blood and water' that flowed from his side signifies, but John tells us that the legs of Jesus weren't broken 'so that the scripture would be fulfilled' (verse 36; see Psalm 34:20).

Joseph of Arimathea

We don't know with any certainty where Arimathea was situated. Luke tells us that it was a 'city of the Jews' (Luke 23:51). It is possible that it was another name for Ramathaim-Zophim (1 Samuel 1:1). John tells us that Joseph was a secret disciple (verse 38), while Matthew seems to suggest that he had just become a disciple (Matthew 27:57); the other gospel writers tell us that he was 'waiting for the kingdom of God' (Mark 15:43; Luke 23:51). So Joseph was either a secret disciple, a new believer or an 'almost believer' to use one of the Reformers' favourite descriptions.

With Pilate's permission Joseph and Nicodemus take the body and prepare it for the grave 'in accordance with the Jewish burial custom' (verse 40). This involved a linen sheet and an ointment made from sweet-smelling spices. If the preparation was quite normal, the amount of spices certainly wasn't. The measurement mentioned here is a *litra* which was 327.45 grams. So seventy-five of these would be a little over 24.5kg which was enough for the burial of a king (cf. 2 Chronicles 16:14). Perhaps that was the point that John was making; he certainly goes out of the way to emphasize the sovereignty of Jesus whenever he can.

The idea that Jesus merely fainted on the cross and was revived by the coolness of the tomb is finally put to rest here. There really is no possibility that Jesus survived the beating and the crucifixion, but accepting that he did for a moment, he would have been suffocated by that amount of burial ointment.

John 20:1–18

The resurrection morning

John describes the resurrection from the
point of view of Mary Magdalene.

The first day of the week

All the gospel writers agree on the fundamental facts of the resurrection and that it
took place on 'the first day of the week' (verse 1), that is, the
Sunday after the crucifixion. The word 'week' is 'sabbaths'
which was the way Jews referred to a week; being the time
between two 'sabbaths'.

Mary's surname was 'Magdalene', the feminine form of
Magdala which was the name of one of the towns on the
western shore of the sea of Galilee. Magdala means 'tower' or
'castle' and it is likely that there was a fort or some such
landmark that had given the town its name. Presumably it was
still dark when Mary set out and the sun had begun to rise when
she arrived (Mark 16:2).

The empty tomb

Mary saw that 'the stone had been removed from the entrance'
(verse 1). The verb declares that the stone had been 'lifted up',
implying that it had been taken right out of its groove. The stone
hadn't been merely rolled aside. It couldn't be; it had been
permanently displaced from the place where it should be.
Mary's first instinct was to rush and tell 'Peter and the other
disciple . . . "They have taken the Lord out of the tomb"' (verse
2). These disciples then ran to the tomb.

The 'burial cloth' (verse 7) was a towel or literally a 'sweat cloth' that had been used to tie around the neck and over the head to stop the dead person's mouth falling open. This 'cloth was folded up by itself, separate from the linen'. What is described is a tidy and orderly scene, the opposite to anything that robbers would leave behind. Maybe the head of Jesus passed through the towel and spices in precisely the same way that he would appear in the locked room later (verse 19). The towel was now folded and put aside by itself in a way that declared it wouldn't be needed again. It was the orderliness that caused the other disciple to believe. The language used about the stone and the towel suggests that something significant and miraculous had taken place.

Mary meets Jesus

The two men had looked into the tomb and were convinced by what they saw before Mary arrived. They returned home, but Mary was riveted to the spot by the tragedy of what she thought was a stolen body. For Mary the empty tomb could only mean one thing; that even in death Jesus wasn't allowed to rest in peace. She was utterly devastated and could not contain her grief. She wept and was still weeping when she stooped and looked into the tomb and 'saw two angels in white'.

The word 'angel' means 'messenger' and is used in the Bible to describe both the human and heavenly beings who perform this task on God's behalf. Indeed, often there is no way to distinguish between the two. In this case the fact that they were 'in white' (verse 12) suggests the latter.

The angels and Jesus

The angels ask Mary why she is crying. In the other gospels they assure her that Jesus has risen and perhaps that is what John is implying here. Mary repeats what she had already said, with two striking differences. The words are now intensely personal; he is '*my* Lord' and '*I* do not know where they have put him' (verse 13). It is possible that something in their expressions made Mary turn around to find Jesus standing behind her, although she didn't recognize him at first. This is very strange because tears don't normally hinder our identification of loved ones (verse 15). In almost all the resurrection appearances there is something that limits recognition (cf. Matthew 28:17; Luke 24:13–31, 37; John 21:4). Can it be that resurrection slightly changes a body? That after resurrection, although we are still ourselves, we have been 'changed' in some way (1 Corinthians 15:51)? Jesus asks Mary why she is crying. We have already noticed that to be addressed as 'woman' was not as cold and formal as it sounds to us.

Mary explains, and Jesus replies with the single word, 'Mary' (verse 16), literally 'Miriam'. The word is in its Aramaic form. Mary instantly recognizes him and says, 'Rabboni'. Some translators see a note of affection and render it, 'My dear Master'.

The NIV starts to iron out a problem in what Jesus says next: 'Do not hold on to me'. 'Touch me not' (AV) is the way the old translations express it. There was no reason why Mary shouldn't touch Jesus. In the other accounts the women touch his feet (Matthew 28:9) and soon he would invite Thomas to touch him (verse 27). What Jesus appears to be saying is, 'Mary, don't keep *holding* me *now*. There is plenty of time before I return to the Father'. He adds, 'Go instead to my brothers and tell them.'

Perhaps the lesson we must learn from this is not to hold on to an understanding of Christ that we learned years ago. We need to relate to the living Jesus. Our relationship with him, and our understanding of him, must grow at all times.

Questions

1. What significance is there in the fact that the grave-clothes were 'tidy and orderly'?

2. What is strange about the fact that Mary did not at first recognize Jesus? Why does he tell her not to hold on to him?

3. Imagine you are a barrister, attempting to prove to the court that Jesus really died and rose bodily from death. What evidence would you use? (Your group could make this into a dramatic role play.)

John 20:19–31

The disciples meet the risen Lord

Jesus appears in a locked room and imparts to his disciples the Holy Spirit. Thomas is not convinced by the story but Jesus appears to him individually.

Jesus appears to the disciples (verses 19–23)

We often refer to this room as the 'upper-room', but we have no evidence for that. We know that they gathered later in an upstairs room in Jerusalem (Acts 1:13) and we presume that this was the room they had always used for their meetings. What we do know is that it was 'locked for fear of the Jews'. It is easy to imagine the fear of this small group and how they jumped at every unexplained noise and footfall. If the authorities had gone to such extremes to stop Jesus, surely they would eventually get around to dealing with the disciples in a similar way. Then, suddenly, without a sound Jesus 'stood among them'. He greets them in the usual Jewish way. We have already noticed that 'peace' for the Jew meant much more than it does for us. If any doubt remains in their minds about who he was, it was removed when they saw 'his hands and side' (verse 20). Their joy knew no bounds. Notice:

Their mission

As the Father had sent Jesus, so he now commissions them. 'Sent' is one of the fundamental truths of this gospel. Everything that Jesus had said and done, including his death, was because the Father had *sent* him. In spite of what the Jews could do, it was important that the disciples felt the urgency of getting out of the locked room and being *sent* to a needy world with God's message. As disciples we need to feel that too.

The equipment for their task

The disciples' equipment was the Holy Spirit. There are two quite distinct historical eras of Holy Spirit blessing for God's people. Before Pentecost, the Holy Spirit had been given to individual men and women for special tasks in particular times. After Pentecost (Acts 2:1) every believer is baptized by the Spirit into the body of believers (1 Corinthians 12:13). In these verses Jesus appears to be saying to the disciples, 'Here is the Holy Spirit to equip you for your task until Pentecost, when the whole church will be furnished with a similar blessing.' He, literally, 'expelled a deep breath' and said, 'Receive the Holy Spirit.'

Forgiving and retaining sins

We come to one of the most difficult parts of the teaching of Jesus; it involves forgiving and refusing to forgive (verse 23). This verse is used by some denominations to give their *clergy* authority to forgive and retain sins. But whatever the verse means, it is clear that *all* disciples have the power to do it. The verbs are in the perfect tense and therefore point to a fact that already exists. Surely what these words are saying is that every believer can point to the death of Christ as the basis of forgiveness. If someone accepts the work of the cross, then forgiveness is theirs. If necessary, they can be given assurance of this (1 John 1:9). If they don't accept the work of the cross, then there can be no forgiveness (1 John 5:11).

Jesus and doubtful Thomas (verses 24–29)

Probably in Bible times when twins were born into a family, the first child was named and the other was simply called 'the twin'. This appears to have happened to Thomas. 'Thomas' is a transliteration of the Hebrew for twin (English letters replacing Hebrew) and 'Didymus' is the Greek word for twin. The other writers say little about him, but John paints a picture of a slightly gloomy, intensely practical, no-nonsense disciple. Before the raising of Lazarus Jesus says he is going to Jerusalem and Thomas says, 'Let us also go, that we may die with him' (11:16). In the upper room with the disciples Jesus says to them, 'I am going . . . to prepare a place for you . . . You know the way to the place where I am going' (14:2, 4). But Thomas won't accept this. Unless he knows exactly what is happening, he won't say that he does. So the reaction of Thomas to the resurrection is very important. We know that he will be objective about it.

John notes, 'Thomas . . . one of the Twelve, was not with the disciples when Jesus came' (verse 24). Without Judas there were only eleven and without Thomas there were only ten. But 'the Twelve' is the name of the group and it is retained as the group name even though they aren't all present. All four gospel writers describe the band of disciples in this way.

A week later Jesus 'came and stood among them'. He greets them in the Jewish way, 'Peace be with you!' (verse 26) and invites Thomas to see and touch the evidence. Even though Jesus hadn't been there, he knew exactly what the unbelieving Thomas had demanded. Thomas exclaims, 'My Lord and my God!' (verse 29). This is the first time that anyone in this gospel has acknowledged Jesus like this.

Jesus doesn't say that disciples in the future will be *more* blessed (verse 29). When Jesus was on earth it would have been difficult to believe without seeing, but in our day we don't have the opportunity to see and believe. If we believe, and that is the point, we will be blessed.

The reason why John wrote this gospel (verses 30–31)

This whole document was written with the express purpose that we might be helped to 'believe that Jesus is the Christ' and have 'life in his name' (verse 31). Elsewhere we have defined this as 'the life of God's age' and 'resurrection life'. It is to be enjoyed by being 'born again', which is a work of the Spirit, who applies all the results of Christ's death to us.

Questions

1. In what ways are Christians today 'sent' into the world around them?
2. How has what Jesus says in verse 23 been misunderstood? How then should this verse be interpreted? What are our responsibilities?
3. What do we know about Thomas? Why is the description of how he reacts to the news about the risen Jesus so important for us?

THE EPILOGUE

John 21:1–25

John 21:1–14

Fishing with the boys

After the events of crucifixion and resurrection the disciples return to their former occupation, fishing. This is not necessarily a sign of a return to 'worldly ways' but is certainly the context for Jesus to underline the reality of his resurrection.

 It is easy to see why many think that this gospel originally ended with the conclusion of chapter 20. The final verses of chapter 20 feel like the end of a book, and chapter 21 appears to be an afterthought or postscript. There is no way that we can prove or disprove that chapter 21 was, or was not, part of John's original work. However, it needs to be said that there is no known manuscript that lacks chapter 21, so if chapter 21 was added, it was added at a very early date and most probably by John himself. It could well be that John thought that his gospel needed an epilogue to balance the prologue (1:1–18) at the beginning.

An all-night fishing trip for the boys

The scene shifts to the 'sea of Tiberias' (verse 1). We normally refer to it as the Sea of Galilee. That is how it was known in the days of Jesus, but the development of a new town in AD 20 on the west shore, named after Emperor Tiberius, meant that the inland sea quickly started to be known by that name too.

The small band of disciples had started to break up, so John lists those who were still together (verse 2). Peter wants to stop the group from moping around and dwelling on the past, so he blurts out, 'I'm going out to fish.' His use of the present tense speaks of a continuing activity which is probably why some think that he is saying, 'I'm going back to my old life'. But the context doesn't allow that. All he is saying is, 'I need a breath of fresh air. I'm going fishing. Does anyone want to come with me?' They all respond, 'We'll go with you.' The middle of the verse is slightly mysterious. It says 'they went out', but it doesn't say where they went out *from*. They then got into 'the boat', but John doesn't tell us exactly which boat that was. Was it perhaps the boat they always used for fishing? If it was, then that night's trip was among the most unsuccessful, because 'that night they caught nothing'.

It was literally in the first light of dawn that 'Jesus stood on the shore' (verse 4), but from the boat they did not realize who it was. He calls them, 'Friends' (literally, 'little children'). This word is used not only of an adult (1 John 2:18), but also of a noble-man's son (4:49) and a newly born baby (16:21). It corresponds almost exactly to the English calling fully grown men 'boys' or 'lads'. 'Lads, haven't you got any fish then?' In the language of the New Testament you can ask a question expecting a negative answer. Jesus does that; in other words, he knew they had caught nothing. He told them to throw the net out on the right side of the boat, which they did, and then had difficulty hauling in the net 'because of the large number of fish'.

'It is the Lord!'

The disciple whom Jesus loved said to Peter, 'It is the Lord!' Peter then recognized him too and jumped into the water and swam ashore. 'Lord' is similar to the use of 'Sir' in our society, and sometimes the NIV translates it like that (8:11). It was occasionally used by the disciples to refer to Jesus, but after the resurrection it became the distinctive way of referring to him as the risen Christ.

The outer garment that Peter took off

Peter was stripped for work; he had taken off his tunic to facilitate rowing the boat and hauling in nets. He didn't put it back on before he swam ashore because that would impede him in the water. But he took it with him because it was unthinkable to greet anyone in a state of undress. Jewish law regarded a greeting as a religious act and to do that you had to be clothed.

Bread and breakfast

This whole story illustrates the reality of the resurrection and that must be John's purpose in including it. He had spoken about the empty tomb and Jesus appearing in the locked room, but perhaps he thought he hadn't made it crystal clear that he was talking about a real resurrection body. A mere vision or a spiritual manifestation was hardly likely to have spotted a shoal of fish on the other side of the boat, or to have kindled a charcoal fire on the beach, and it certainly wouldn't have cooked, offered and enjoyed breakfast with them. With hard facts, and the tangible evidence of everyday things, the resurrection is seen to be a reality. It wasn't simply the figment of someone's imagination. If Peter had dreamt that he had seen Jesus after a long night and sleep induced by inactivity, then jumping into the water would have banished the dream and jolted him back to consciousness. But Jesus was still there when he got to the shore, so were the fish, and Jesus personally offered breakfast to the disciples (verse 13).

The great catch

The net was 'full of large fish, 153' (verse 11). From the earliest times commentators have taken great pains in explaining the exact number of fish, and why there were 153 of them. Some have suggested, for example, that 153 was the total number of species of fish known in the ancient world, but this is unfounded. Others point out that 153 is the sum of the numbers 1 to 17. Why seventeen? Well ten is the number of the commandments and seven is the number of the sevenfold gifts of the Spirit. And still others say it is the sum of the numbers symbolized by the letters of Simon's name. But most probably John is saying that in spite of the large number of fish (they had actually counted 153), 'the net was not torn'. John rounds the section off by emphasizing that 'This was now the third time Jesus appeared to his disciples after he was raised from the dead' (verse 14).

Questions

1. Why does John choose to include this account in his gospel?
2. Why does he specify the number of fish that were caught? What benefit is there for us in any of these possible explanations?
3. Jesus meets his disciples at their work. How would you advise a modern Christian trawlerman to relate his work to the presence of Jesus, in the face of dwindling fish stocks, fierce competition, international laws etc.?

Peter's restoration as pastor

Peter had denied his Lord. Will he be replaced or restored? The Good Shepherd graciously renews his commission to a penitent under-shepherd.

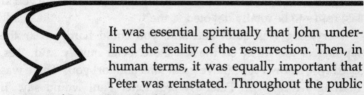

It was essential spiritually that John underlined the reality of the resurrection. Then, in human terms, it was equally important that Peter was reinstated. Throughout the public ministry of Jesus, Peter had been the natural leader and pastor of the small band of disciples. One reason why the band had started to break up could have been the lack of leadership and influence of a pastor. The group had always looked to Peter and he hadn't failed them, although in a moment of crisis he had failed his master. Would Jesus reinstate Peter or replace him? The occasion is marked as important and solemn by both John and Jesus using two slightly different full names for Peter. First he is 'Simon Peter' then 'Simon, son of John' (verse 15).

When they had finished eating Jesus said to him, 'Do you truly love me more than these?' As Jesus spoke, he may have been pointing at the other disciples, but it is much more likely that his hand swept over the boat and all the other fishing equipment. Was Peter ready to give up a steady and secure job and now devote himself whole-heartedly to Jesus and his work?

Jesus' questions and Peter's response

In a very simplified form, and allowing a little dramatic licence, you could suggest that the scene on the beach happened like this:

Jesus spoke first. 'Simon son of John, are you really devoted to me now?'

Peter's eyes dropped to the charcoal fire where the fish had been cooked and he remembered the brazier outside the high priest's house and his mind again filled with the pain of denial. He knew he couldn't hide anything from Jesus. 'Lord, you know I have the greatest affection for you.'

Jesus said, 'Feed my lambs.'

Again Jesus said to Peter, 'Simon, the bottom line is, are you at last ready to be totally devoted to me?'

Everything was quiet and still; you could hardly hear the lapping of the water on the sea-shore. Peter quietly said, 'Yes, Lord, you know I love (have great affection for) you.' There was nothing wrong with Peter's word. Later Paul would say, 'If anyone does not love (it is the same word) the Lord – a curse be on him' (1 Corinthians 16:22).

Jesus said, 'Shepherd my sheep.'

A third time Jesus said, 'Simon, son of John, do you love me?' (Jesus now used the same word as Peter.) The first question had challenged the superiority of Peter's love for his Lord over his love for the fishing business. The second examined the reality of it. The final question confronted Peter's claim to have an affectionate love for Christ.

Peter was hurt by the question. Yet he looked directly at Jesus and answered, 'Lord, you know all things. You know I have great affection and nothing but friendly love for you.'

'Tend my sheep,' Jesus said.

Peter has passed the test with flying colours.

Peter's denial is wiped away

Peter had denied Jesus three times (18:15–18, 25–27); now he is given three opportunities to declare his love for Christ. In three decisive strokes the memory of the denials are wiped away; the slate was clean once more. Before a charcoal fire he had made three denials. Now, before the same sort of fire, he makes three confessions of love and receives three commissions. The restoration is complete.

The commissioning of Pastor Peter

The flock is described in different ways; either as 'lambs' (verse 15) or 'sheep' (verses 16–17). John doesn't have specific people in mind, he is describing the flock in the widest possible terms. Peter's function was to 'feed' them – the word is talking about 'grazing' – and he is also to 'take care' of them. So Peter was commissioned to shepherd and oversee the flock, providing both fodder and care.

The prophecy about his future

Note the formula 'I tell you the truth' (verse 18), so we know that the prophecy is important, but its meaning is enigmatic. Two things are contrasted: the freedom of youth and the restrictions of old age, Peter's old age. With hindsight our minds jump to the restraint of crucifixion and that seems to be what John has in mind (verse 19). The prophecy is followed by a call to follow Christ in the present tense; so it has the force of 'Keep on following.'

Questions

1. Why does Jesus ask Peter about his love for him three times? Try to imagine what Peter felt like and share your feelings with the group?
2. What, specifically, is Peter commissioned to do? What does this mean? What can we learn from this about the functions of Christian leadership?
3. What exactly is 'Christian love' and how does it differ from any other kind? Does either of these statements help: 'Love is wanting the other person near you'; 'Love is wanting the best for the other person even if you don't like him/her'?

Problems with the different words for 'love'

The Greek of the New Testament is far richer than English as far as the verb 'to love' is concerned, there being several verbs for our one. It is extremely difficult to express these differences exactly and almost every scholar you consult will have their own way of doing so. The matter is further complicated by:

▶ The words were originally spoken in Aramaic, the local Hebrew dialect, so they have already gone through one translation to appear in the New Testament.

▶ John, the writer of this gospel, or whoever translated it into Greek for the New Testament, wasn't consistent in the words he used. The questions of Jesus and the replies of Peter involve two different words for 'love'. The translators of the NIV try to show the difference by rendering one word 'truly love' (verses 15–16) and the other simply 'love' (verses 15–17). But it is difficult to argue that one word was stronger and the other weaker. When one of the disciples is described as 'the disciple whom Jesus loved', both words are used on different occasions (cf. 13:23 and 20:2). In all the other passages where love is mentioned the words are used interchangeably. There is a slender possibility that when the words are used together, as in this passage, one word is slightly more altruistic and the other more physically affectionate.

Jesus and the disciple he loved

The role of the 'disciple whom Jesus loved' is revealed and the gospel ends appropriately with a focus on the greatness of Jesus.

The focus now moves to 'the disciple whom Jesus loved' (verse 20). We can now make our choice from the very tiny group (verse 2), with the help of some clues from the last supper (13:23–25). There is little doubt that it is John, the writer of this gospel. So the one writing all these details is one who has had the intimacy of having 'leaned back against Jesus' (verse 20).

Peter is obviously worried about what is going to happen to John. Jesus makes it clear to Peter, 'If I want him to remain alive until I return, what is that to you?' (verse 22). The NIV draws out the meaning – 'remains alive' – and that is what Jesus has in mind although he just says, 'remains' (cf. 1 Corinthians 15:16). John must do what Christ wants him to do and Peter must do the same. For Peter this was to follow Christ. The 'you' is emphatic: '*You* must follow me,' Jesus says to him.

So we have two different areas of concentration. Peter must be single-minded about being the shepherd of the sheep and in the end about dying for Christ, while John's function must be as a witness to the life of Christ, living to an old age and in the end dying in peace. And this passage really makes it clear that this is what John did. It is a reminder for all disciples that we must get on with what Christ has given us to do.

The limitless Christ

The final two verses are written by someone other than the author, but someone who knew that John's testimony was valid (verse 24). The gospel ends on the marvellous note of the limitlessness of the work of Christ (verse 25). Perhaps we need to remind ourselves again of the words at the end of the previous chapter. These words 'are written that (we) may believe that Jesus is the Christ, the Son of God, and that by believing (we) may have life in his name.'

Questions

1. How far should we be concerned about what God requires of others and how far should we mind our own business? Suggest some guidelines.
2. In your studies in John's gospel what have you learned about your church, its good points and bad? Make a list (or two lists!).
3. The sub-title of this Bible guide is 'Find the way'. How far have your studies helped you to find your way?

Further reading

B. Milne, *The Message of John*, Bible Speaks Today (IVP, 1993).

R. V. G. Tasker, *The Gospel according to St John*, Tyndale New Testament Commentary (IVP, 1960).

For preachers and teachers, a major commentary based on the *New International Version* of the Bible:

D. A. Carson, *The Gospel according to John* (IVP, 1991).

HOUSEGROUPS

the leaders' survival guide

Editors: Ian Coffey and Stephen Gaukroger

Ever since New Testament times small groups of Christians have met to learn, to worship and to grow together. Housegroups have enjoyed great popularity in the last few decades, and much experience and wisdom in leading them has been distilled by the authors of this book.

Are you thinking of starting a housegroup or taking your existing group forward? Or has your group gone a little flat? *Housegroups: the leaders' survival guide* will give you the vision you are looking for:

* ★ What's the point of housegroups?
* ★ What makes a good leader?
* ★ Teaching the Bible in small groups
* ★ Prayer, worship and evangelism
* ★ Troubleshooter's guide and much more

Authors include Peter Meadows, John Earwicker, Dave Cave, Steve Motyer, Nick Mercer, Chris Bowater.

Editors Stephen Gaukroger and Ian Coffey are both senior ministers in Baptist churches and series editors of the Crossway Bible Guides. They share with the other authors a contagious enthusiasm for housegroups.

JOSHUA

Charles Price

Free to follow

Crossway Bible Guides

Joshua is a book about God! He is revealed as a God of action in the cut and thrust of real life. Joshua shows God:

* dealing with real conflict
* undergirding real disappointment
* restoring after real failure
* operating in real people

From Joshua we learn not only that God is indispensable; he is available to those who are available to him and follow him.

Crossway Bible Guides are designed for personal devotion and for group study leaders and members. They give a concise summary and lively application of each passage. They help us grasp the message of the Bible, and, more important, help the Bible get a grip on us.

A useful resource for personal Bible reading and group studies –   Michael Green

Evangelical Alliance is delighted to join together with Crossway in publishing this new series –   Clive Calver

Individuals or groups could find great benefit from this series. Major points are highlighted followed by uncompromising and sharp questions –   Donald English

These guides will facilitate, stimulate and enrich your discovery of God's Word –   Roger Forster

Charles Price is an experienced Bible teacher with a ministry that takes him all over the world. He is based at Capernwray Hall in Lancashire, where he lives with his wife Hilary.